YOU CAN TEACH YOURSELF® ROCK GUITAR

By William Bay and Mark Lonergan

You Can Teach Yourself Rock Guitar is a unique, new guitar method designed to help you learn contemporary music. Upon completion of this method, the student should be able to handle the demands of most contemporary rock music. In addition, the student wil develop the ability to hear and appreciate a wide variety of contemporary harmonic colors and rhythms.

CD CONTENTS*

1. Tuning {2:11}
2. Basic Blues Song {:48}
3. Our First Blues Lead Solo {1:08}
4. The Slide {:13}
5. Blues Slide Solo {1:01}
6. Hammer-On {:58}
7. Hammer-On Solo {:59}
8. Pull-Off {:53}
9. Pull-Off Solo {:59}
10. Combining Effects Solo {1:01}
11. Vibrato {:58}
12. Blues Solo With Vibrato {1:00}
13. The Bend {:55}
14. Overdrive {1:03}
15. Key of E Solo #1 {1:42}
16. Key of E Solo #2 {1:08}
17. Key of E Solo #3 {1:26}
18. E Chord Study {1:16}
19. Blues Rhythm Shuffle Pt. 1 {:22}
20. Blues Rhythm Shuffle Pt. 2 {:17}
21. Blues Rhythm Shuffle Pt. 3 {:18}
22. Putting It All Together {1:28}
23. Blues Pattern 1 {:58}
24. Blues Pattern 2 {:23}
25. Blues Pattern 3 {:25}
26. Blues Pattern 4 {:28}
27. 16 G's {1:02}
28. Key of G Solo 1 {1:07}
29. Key of G Solo 2 {1:08}

30. Key of G Solo 3 {1:07}
31. G Chord Study {1:16}
32. Drivin' D {:44}
33. Key of D Solo 1 {1:13}
34. Key of D Solo 2 {1:08}
35. Key of D Solo 3 {1:15}
36. D Chord Study #1 {1:02}
37. D Chord Study #2 {:25}
38. Do It {:47}
39. Key of A Solo #1 {1:05}
40. Key of A Solo #2 {1:08}
41. Key of A Solo #3 {1:13}
42. A Chord Study {1:00}
43. Power Riff {:17}
44. Grand Slam {1:00}
45. Key of C Solo #1 {:59}
46. Key of C Solo #2 {1:08}
47. Key of C Solo #3 {1:05}
48. C Chord Study {1:02}
49. Rhythm Break {:49}
50. Down Shift {1:00}
51. Key of F Solo #1 {1:25}
52. Key of F Solo #2 {1:15}
53. Key of F Solo #3 {1:23}
54. F Chord Study #1 {1:17}
55. F Chord Study #2 {1:16}
56. Funk Drive {1:02}
57. Key of Bb Solo #1 {1:07}
58. Key of Bb Solo #2 {1:13}

59. Key of Bb Solo #3 {1:06}
60. Bb Chord Study {1:21}
61. Pentatonic Scale {:24}
62. Example 1 {:25}
63. Example 2 {:19}
64. Example 3 {:22}
65. Example 4 {:19}
66. Example 5 {:19}
67. Example 6 {:38}
68. Example 7 & 8 {:40}
69. Example 10 {:34}
70. Example 11 {:41}
71. Example 12 {:33}
72. Example 13 {:37}
73. Example 14 {:20}
74. Example 15 {:18}
75. Example 17 {:26}
76. Example 19 {1:16}
77. Example 20 {:33}
78. Example 21 {:25}
79. Example 22 {:22}
80. Example 23 {:22}
81. Example 24 {:43}
82. Example 25 {:24}
83. Example 26 {:17}
84. Example 27 {:17}
85. Example 28 {:21}
86. Example 29 {1:13}

*This book is available as a book only or as a book/compact

1 2 3 4 5 6 7 8 9 0

© 1992 BY MEL BAY PUBLICATIONS, INC., PACIFIC, MO 63069.
ALL RIGHTS RESERVED. INTERNATIONAL COPYRIGHT SECURED. B.M.I. MADE AND PRINTED IN U.S.A.

Visit us on the Web at www.melbay.com — E-mail us at email@melbay.com

Table of Contents

Upon completion of this course, we recommend Mel Bay's *Complete Rock Guitar Book* (MB94560) as a further course of instruction.

SECTION ONE

BY WILLIAM BAY

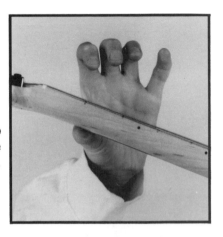

#1

Place your thumb in the middle of the back of the neck.

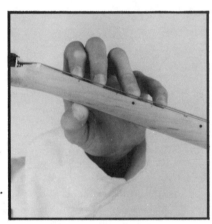

#2

Place your fingers FIRMLY on the string DIRECTLY BEHIND THE FRETS.

The correct way to hold the guitar.

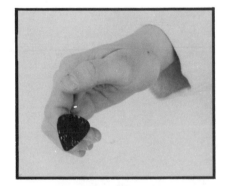

#2

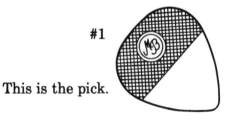

#1

This is the pick.

#3

Hold it in this manner, firmly between the thumb and first finger.

Time Signature

4/4 or **C** time = four counts per measure.

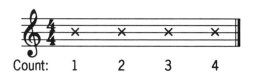

Count: 1   2   3   4

Notes and Rests

Whole Note (Play)	**Whole Rest (Rest — Do Not Play)**
o	▬
Four Counts	Four Counts
Half Note	**Half Rest**
↓	▬
Two Counts	Two Counts
Quarter Note	**Quarter Rest**
↓	𝄽
One Count	One Count
Eighth Note	**Eighth Rest**
♪ or ♫	𝄾
One Half Count	One Half Count

Count and clap the following exercise.

Count: 1 2 3 4   1 2 3 4   1 2 3 4   1   2   3   4   1 2 3 4

STARTING POINT — BASIC BLUES RHYTHM

Tap your guitar and count:

×   ×   ×   ×

one   two three four

Now, say the word "Am-ster-dam." Notice the rhythmic sound. We call this a triplet. Divide each count into three taps (or a triplet) and try the following:

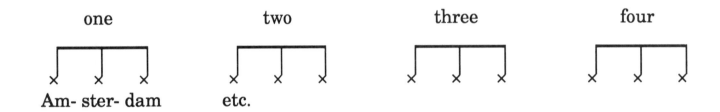

When you have the above triplet rhythm down, try tying the first two taps together. Listen to the tape and try this rhythm known as "the blues shuffle":

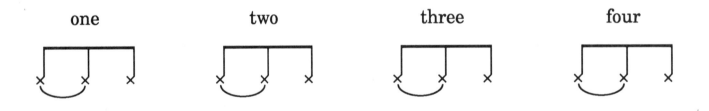

Or, as written in music notation:

TUNING YOUR GUITAR

To tune your guitar, listen to the companion recording and tune up as follows:

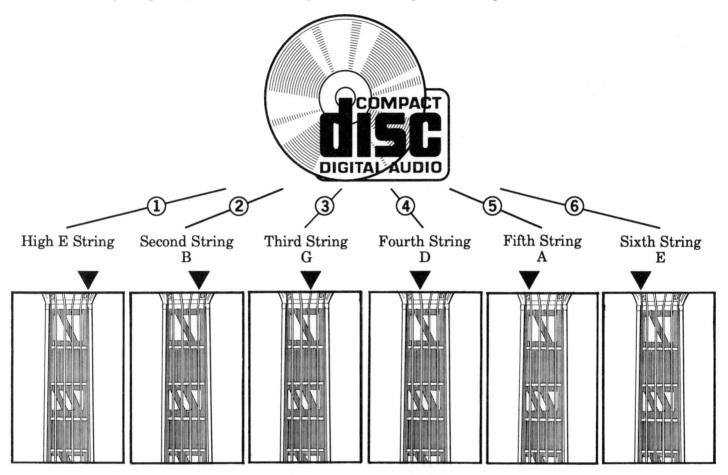

| High E String | Second String
B | Third String
G | Fourth String
D | Fifth String
A | Sixth String
E |

Basic Blues Song

The following song has 12 measures. Listen to it on the recording. We will soon learn solo notes to go with various parts of the basic blues progression.

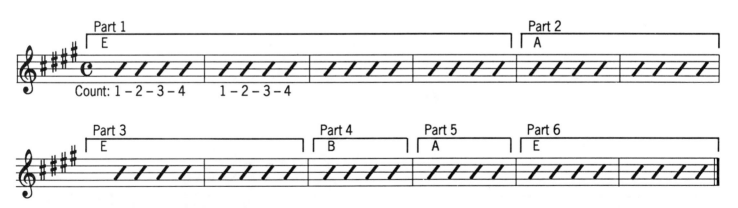

PREPARATORY SOLO STUDIES

The following notes will serve as building blocks for lead guitar solos:

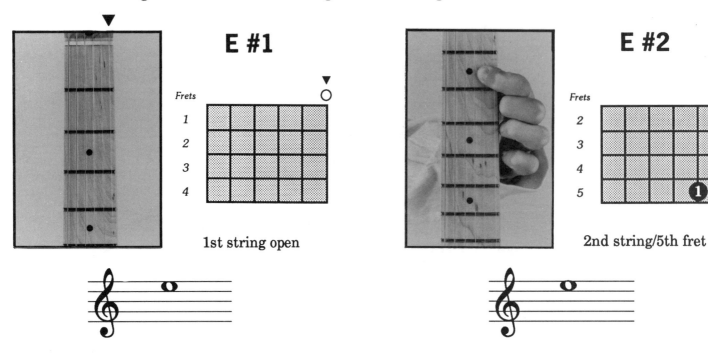

E #1

Frets
1
2
3
4

1st string open

E #2

Frets
2
3
4
5

2nd string/5th fret

High E

Frets
9
10
11
12

1st string/12th fret

E #1, E #2, and high E will be used with Parts 1, 3, and 6 of our basic blues songs.

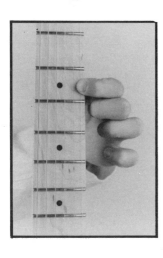

A

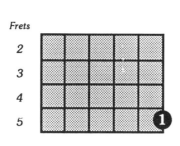

Frets
2
3
4
5

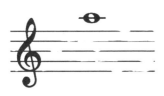

1st string/5th fret

High A

Frets
14
15
16
17

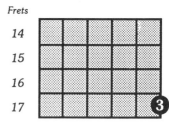

1st string/17th fret

A and high A will be used with Parts 2 and 5 of our basic blues song.

B

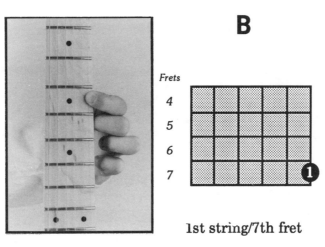

Frets
4
5
6
7

1st string/7th fret

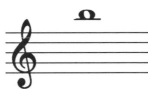

B will be used with Part 4 of our basic blues song.

Our First Blues Lead Solo

Play the following solo with the tape:

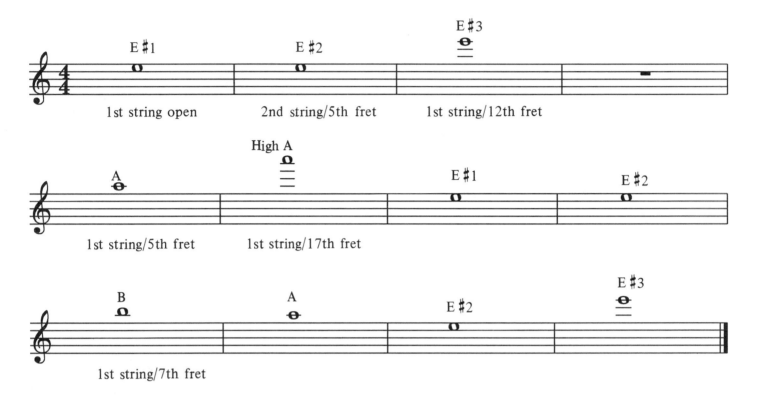

E ♯1 — 1st string open
E ♯2 — 2nd string/5th fret
E ♯3 — 1st string/12th fret

A — 1st string/5th fret
High A — 1st string/17th fret
E ♯1
E ♯2

B — 1st string/7th fret
A
E ♯2
E ♯3

Practice the above solo until you can play it easily.

THE SLIDE

The slide is our first effect. The symbol for a slide is this: ╱ To slide into a note, finger a note two frets lower than the note you want to play. Then, after you pick the lower note, quickly slide up to the desired note *without* picking the string again.

For example, to slide into E ♯2:   Pick this note   and then without lifting your finger *and* without picking again slide into E ♯2.

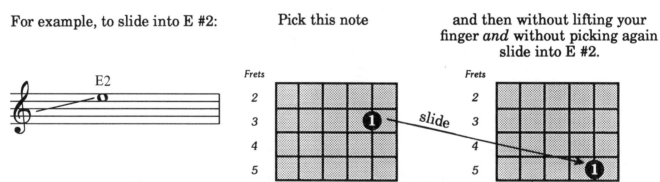

Blues Slide Solo

Play our basic blues solo again, this time using the slide effect as shown. Play with the tape.

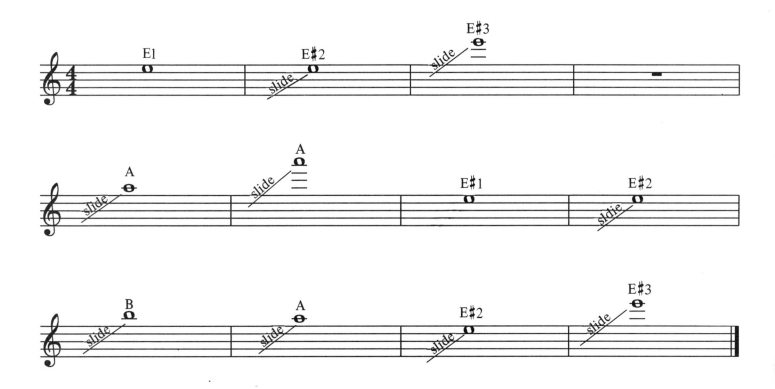

Practice the above slide solo until you have it mastered!

"HAMMER-ON" EFFECT

This is a very important effect for rock lead guitar. To accomplish this effect, you pick one note. Then, without raising your left-hand finger and without picking the string again, you press down hard on a higher note on the same string with a different finger. Usually the first note is fingered with the index finger of your left hand, and the second note is fingered with the left-hand ring finger.

A hammer-on looks like this:

Here is how you play the hammer-on using the notes we have learned:

E #2

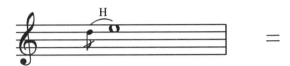

=

① Finger second string, 3rd fret, with the first finger and pick the note.

② Keep first finger down on string and quickly press third finger down on the 5th fret.

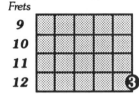

High E

=

① Finger first string, 10th fret, with the first finger and pick the note.

② While first finger remains pressed down, press third finger down on the 12th fret.

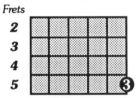

A

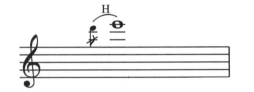

=

① Finger first string, 3rd fret, with the first finger and pick the note.

② While first finger remains pressed down, press third finger down on the 5th fret.

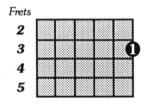

High A

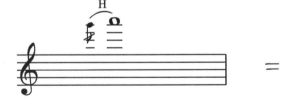

=

① Finger first string, 15th fret, with the first finger and pick the note.

② While first finger remains pressed down, press third finger down on the 17th fret.

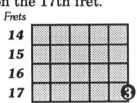

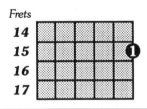

B

=

① Finger first string, 5th fret, with the first finger and pick the note.

② While first finger remains pressed down, press third finger down on the 7th fret.

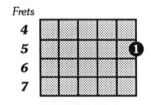

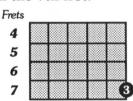

Our Basic Blues Solo Using Hammer-On

Play with the tape.

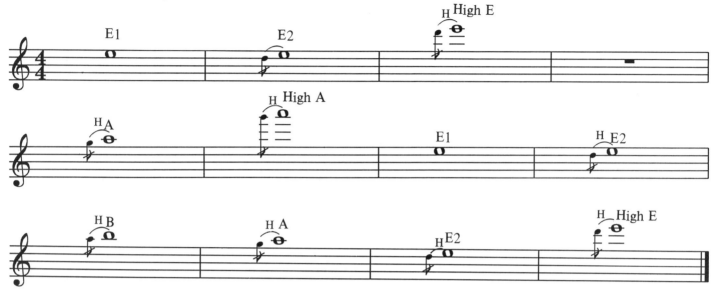

A pull-off looks like this:

A pull-off works in just the opposite way from that of a hammer-on. To play a pull-off, play the higher note first (third finger) and then, while the third finger is still on the higher note, press your first finger down on the desired note (usually 2 frets down). Then pull your first finger off of the string with a snapping motion. This will allow the first-finger note to sound (without picking the string again).

Thus, **Step One**

Play higher note.

Step Two

While higher note is sounding, press first finger down on lower note.

Step Three

Pull third finger off of string and let first-finger note sound.

PULL-OFF CHART

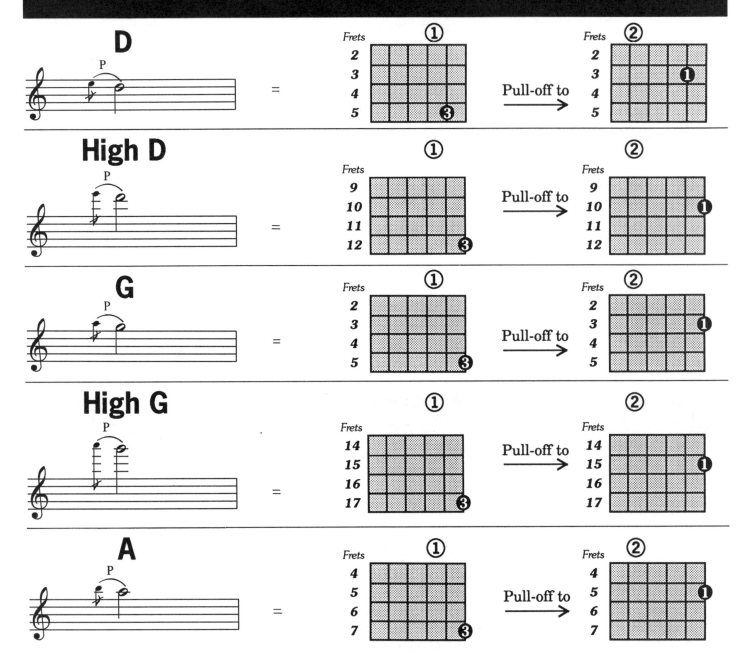

Pull-Off Solo

Notice that on this solo we play each note for only *two* counts! Play with the tape.

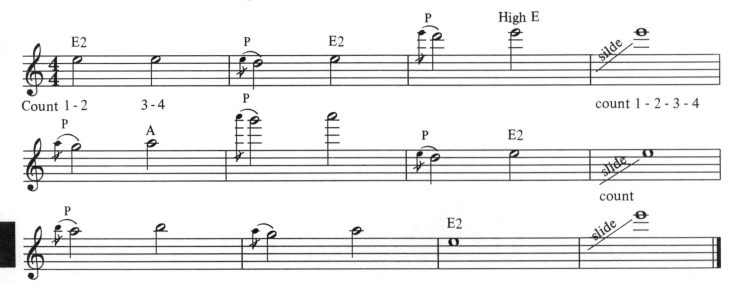

Count 1 - 2   3 - 4   count 1 - 2 - 3 - 4

count

COMBINING EFFECTS

Frequently, rock lead guitarists combine the hammer-on and the pull-off. In other words, you can hammer-on to a note and immediately pull-off back to the original note; or, you can pull-off down to a note and then quickly hammer-on back to the original pitch.

The following solo uses combined effects. Play with the tape.

Rock Solo

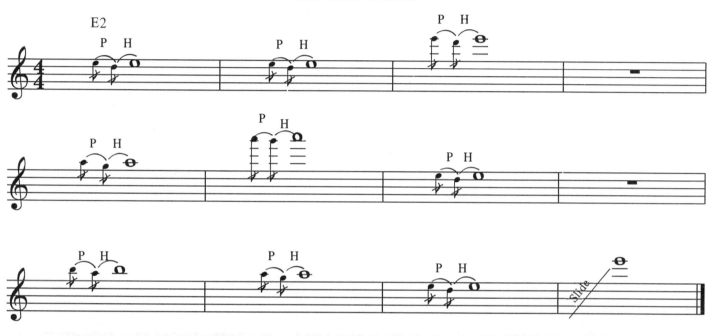

VIBRATO

Vibrato is a great blues/rock lead guitar effect. It looks like this: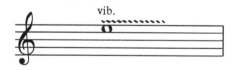

The most widely used method of vibrato is to play a note and then, while you are still holding your left-hand finger down, rock your left hand back and forth (toward the tuning keys and then toward the tailpiece).

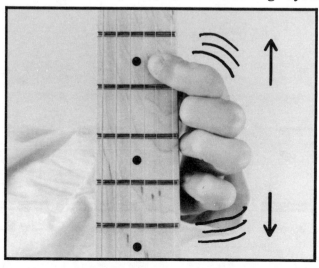

Vibrato Practice

Practice the vibrato technique on the following notes:

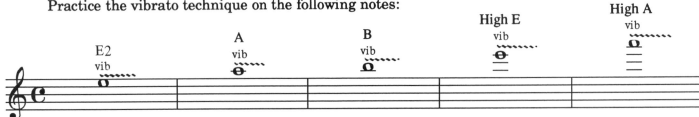

Blues Slide Solo with Vibrato

Now let's play the blues slide solo played earlier, but let's add vibrato to the notes as shown. Practice with the tape.

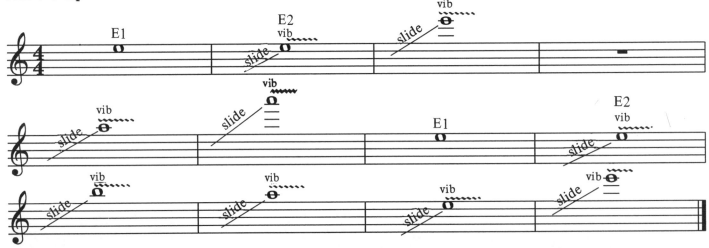

NOTE VALUE REVIEW

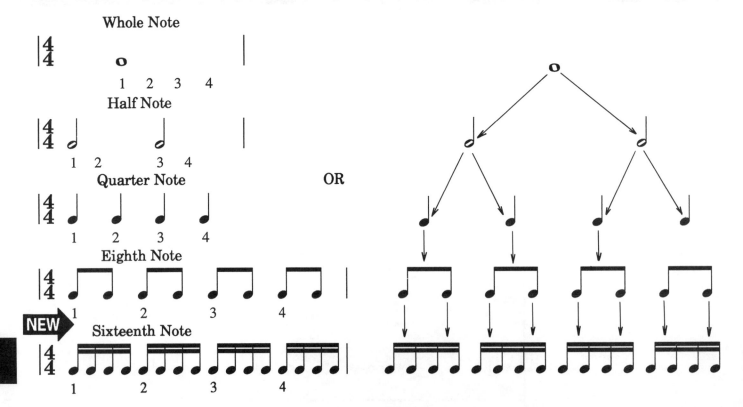

Whole Note

Half Note

Quarter Note   OR

Eighth Note

NEW ➤ Sixteenth Note

LEARNING TO READ TABLATURE

Tablature is a way of writing guitar music which tells you where to find notes. In tablature:

> ## Lines = Strings
> ## Numbers = Frets

Lines = Strings

Numbers = Frets

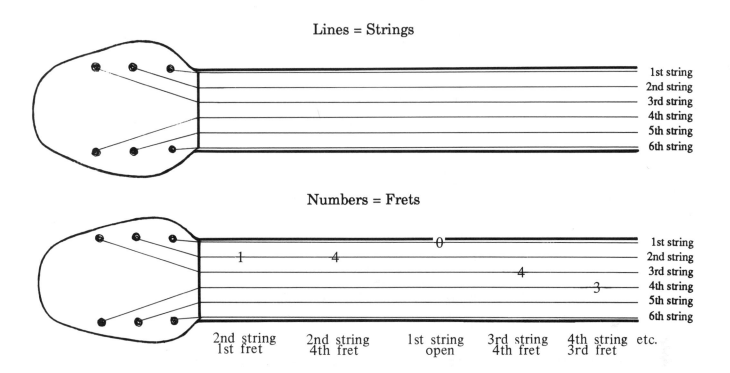

When numbers appear right above one another, more than one note is played at the same time.

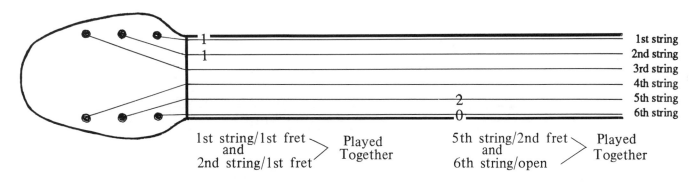

Learning to bend notes is essential to blues/rock lead guitar. To bend a note, finger your note and then push the string towards the sixth string. This raises the pitch. (You will need very light-gauge strings on your guitar to bend notes effectively. Also, you will see that it is easier to bend notes the higher you go up the fingerboard.)

A bend looks like this on your guitar:

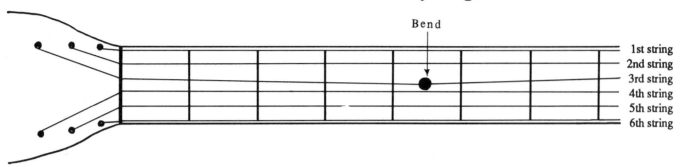

A bend is notated like this:

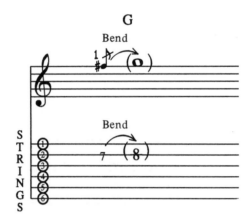

In the above example, you would play second string, 7th fret, and bend the string until the note sounds like the note on second string, 8th fret.

Practice bending these notes:

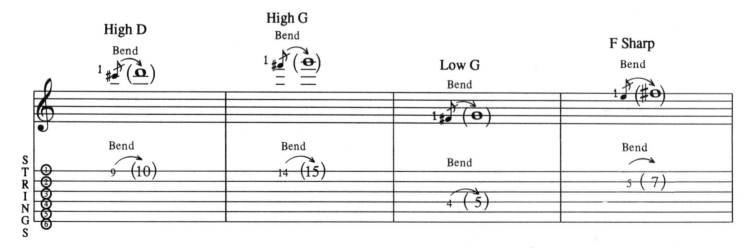

Note: In order to bend notes easily, you must have extra-light gauge or "rock-gauge" strings on your guitar.

KEY OF E

In each key, we will now learn:
1. A "driving bass" solo
2. Three solos based on popular licks
3. Power chords
4. Rock rhythm studies
5. Scale patterns for improvisation

Driving Bass Solo / Key of E

Notes needed:

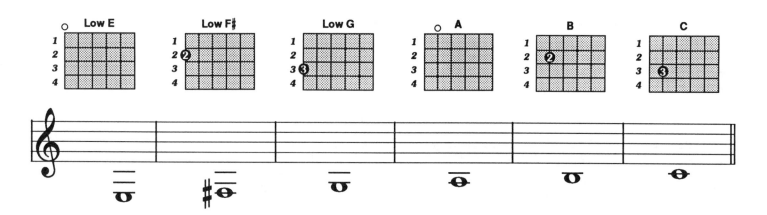

Note: ♩‿♩ means to hold two notes together.

Overdrive

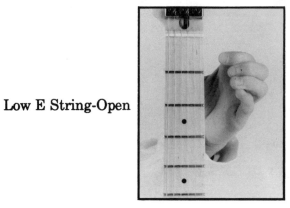

Low E String-Open

Fingerboard position of left hand

Lick #1

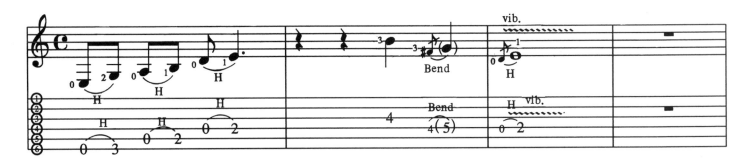

Lick #2

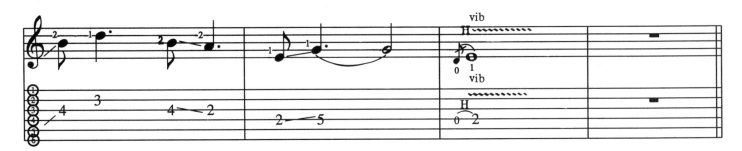

(1) Memorize Licks #1 and #2.

(2) To play with the recording, play Lick #1 twice and then play Lick #2.

Solo #1

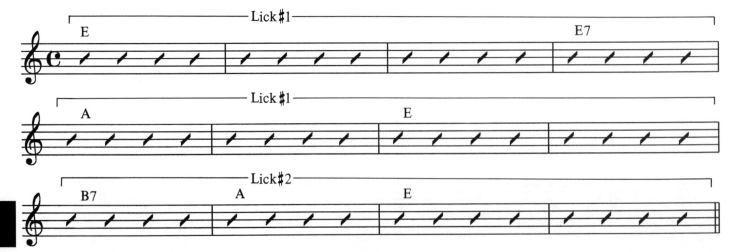

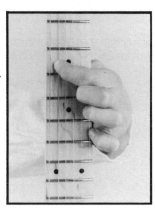

5th string   Fingerboard
1st finger   position of
7th fret   left hand

Lick #1

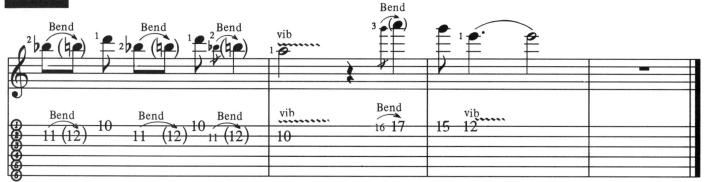

Lick #2

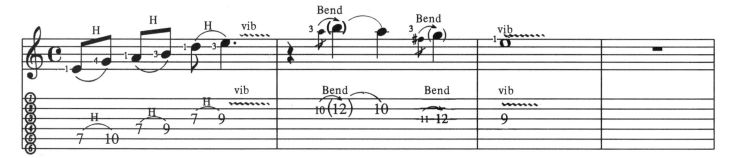

① Memorize Licks #1 and #2.

② To play with the recording, play Lick #1 twice and then play Lick #2.

Solo #2

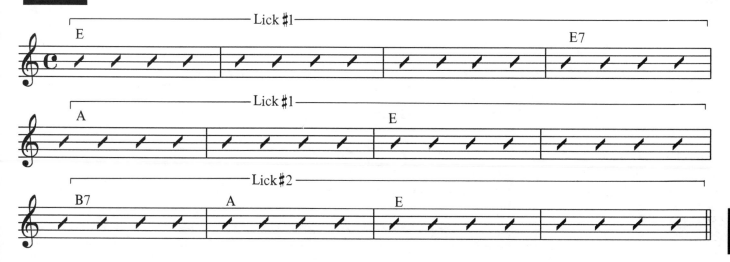

This solo utilizes a rhythm called "triplets." Triplets are a group of three notes. They are frequently taught like this:

Say → Am-ster-dam or one trip-let

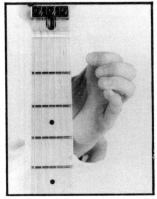

Fingerboard position of left hand

Low E / Open

Listen to the tape to get the feeling of the rock triplet.

Lick #1 This lick starts with "pick-up notes."

Play four times.

Lick #2

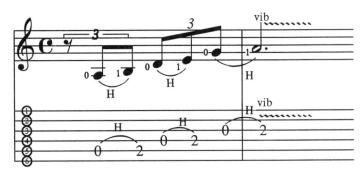

Lick #3

① Memorize Licks #1, #2, and #3.

② To play with the recording, play Lick #1 four times. Then play Lick #2 twice. Next, play Lick #1 twice. Then play Lick #3 once. End by playing Lick #1 twice.

Solo #3

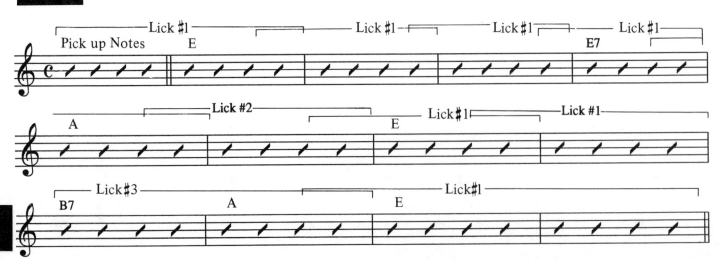

GUIDE TO CHORD DIAGRAMS

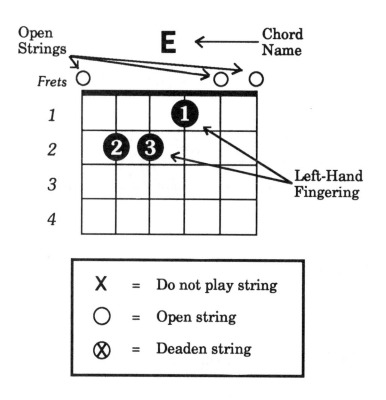

Open Strings

E ← Chord Name

Frets

1

2

3

4

Left-Hand Fingering

X	=	Do not play string
O	=	Open string
⊗	=	Deaden string

Types of Chords

On the next page you will see a master reference listing of types of chords used in the key of E. The chords are broken into two types — full chords and "power chords." The type of chord selected depends on the sound you want to get. The power chords give less notes but work well with heavy amplification. See what works best for you!

Reference Chord Table

E Major

Full Chords | Power Chords

E7

Full Chords | Power Chords

A

Full Chords | Power Chords

B7

Full Chords | Power Chords

E Chord Study #1

Listen to the rhythm on the tape. Practice on your own, then try to play with the recording.

Basic Rhythm

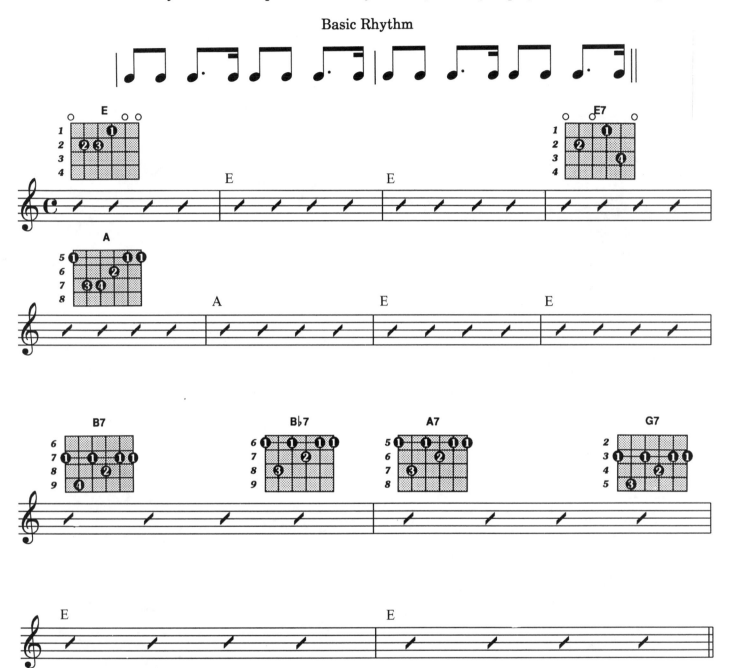

Now try the above study using the following power-chord forms:

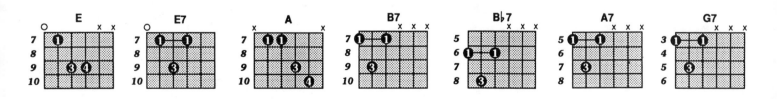

Blues Rhythm Shuffle

Part 1

This is the basic building block for blues and rock guitar. We will learn it a section at a time. Listen to the tape to get the rhythm down. Notice that we play two notes at the same time.

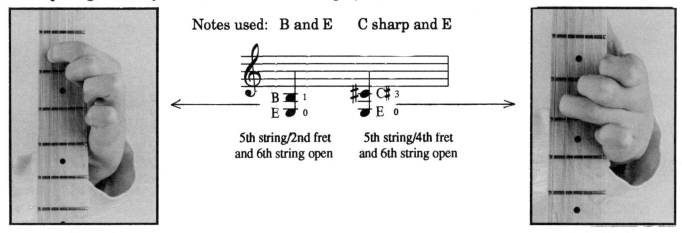

Notes used: B and E   C sharp and E

B ... 1   C♯ 3
E ... 0   E 0

5th string/2nd fret   5th string/4th fret
and 6th string open   and 6th string open

Listen to the tape — then play Part 1 until you know it.

Part 1

Part 2

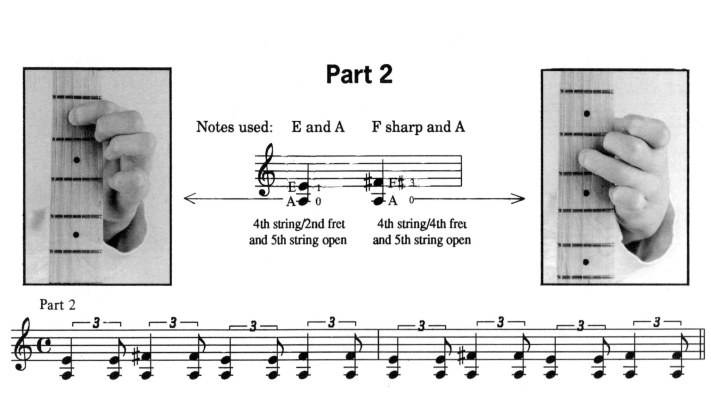

Notes used: E and A   F sharp and A

E ... 1   F♯ 3
A ... 0   A 0

4th string/2nd fret   4th string/4th fret
and 5th string open   and 5th string open

Part 2

Part 3

This part is harder because you must stretch your hand. Remember, for Parts 2 and 3, you play only notes on the fourth and fifth strings.

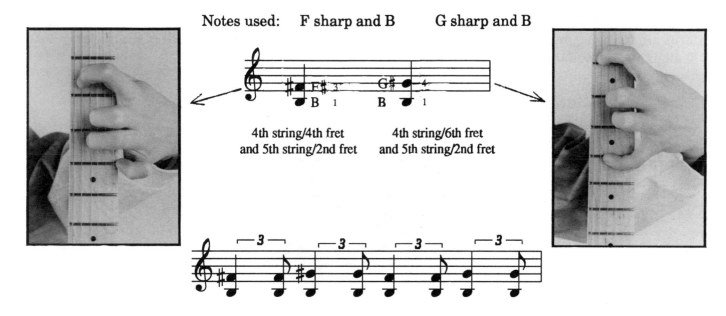

Putting It All Together
Rock/Blues Rhythm Shuffle

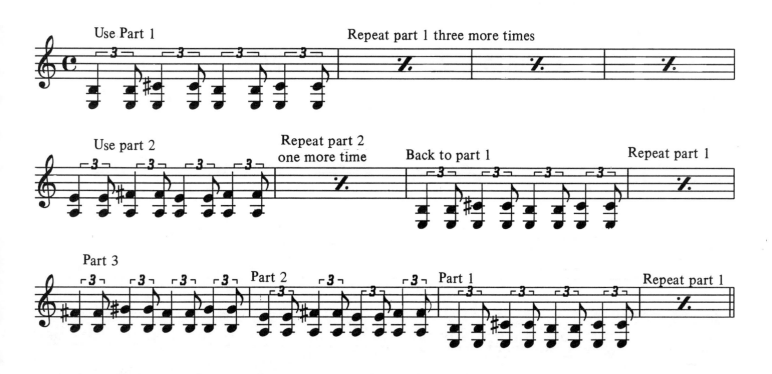

Basic Blues Runs

In blues and rock, basic fingerboard patterns exist which are the basis of solos and improvising. These patterns are the same in any key except that you will move them up or down the neck of the guitar. Practice them going up and coming down.

Pattern #1 — Open Position

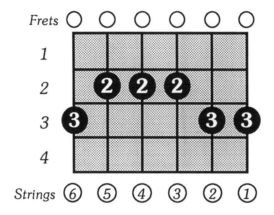

Practice the following pattern going up and coming down. First, play each note with a down pick motion (⊓). Next, try *alternate picking*. This is where you pick one note down and the next up, etc.

⊓ = down pick   V = up pick

Pattern #1 — Open Position

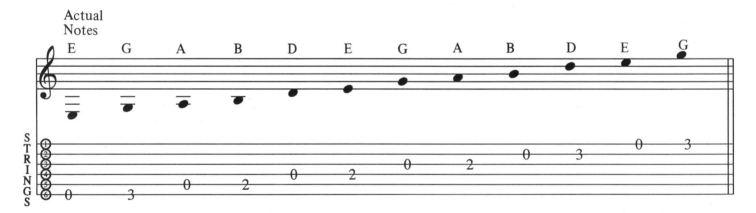

Remember, you can use any note in this or the subsequent E patterns to improvise when you are playing in the key of E.

E Blues Pattern #2

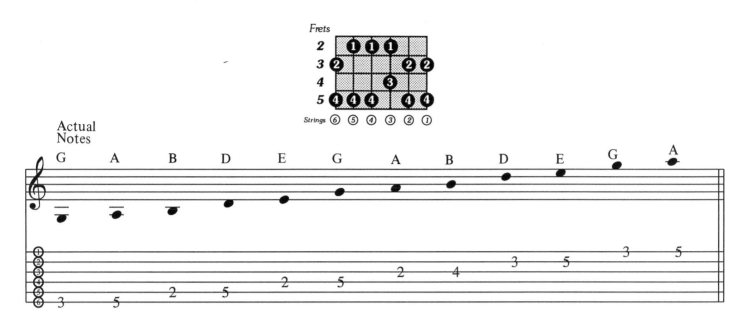

E Blues Pattern #3

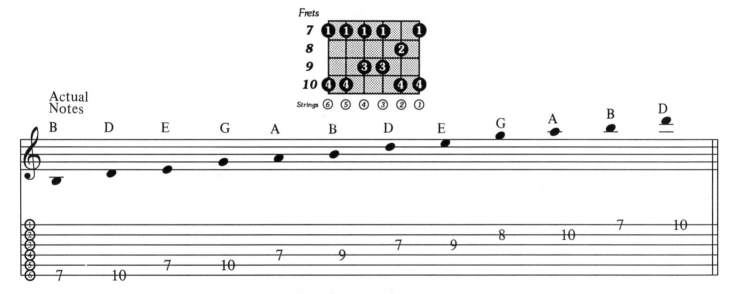

E Blues Pattern #4

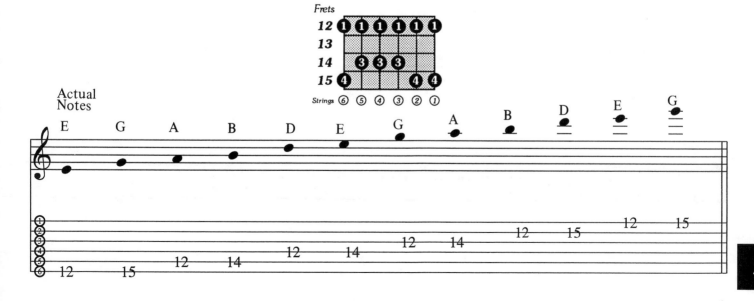

Driving Bass Solo / Key of G

Notes needed:

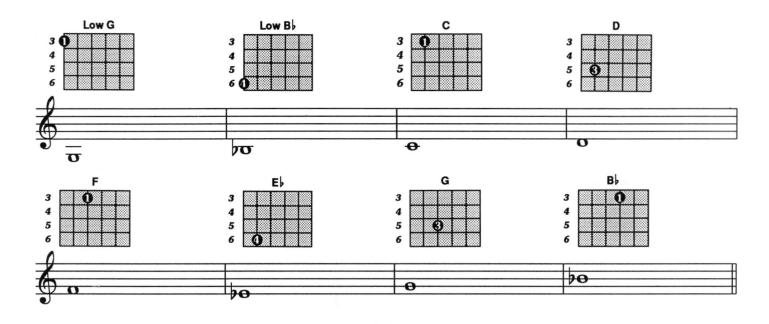

16 G's

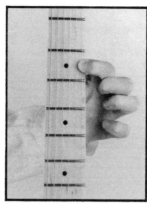

1st string
1st finger
3rd fret

Fingerboard
position of
the left hand

Lick #1

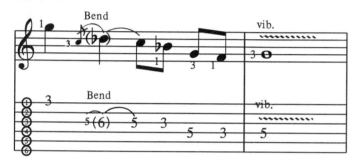

Lick #2

Lick #3

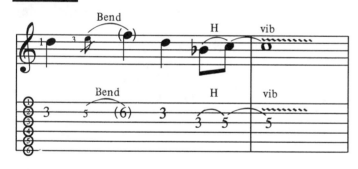

① Memorize Licks #1, #2, and #3.

② To play with the recording, play Lick #1 twice and Lick #2 once. Play Lick #1 again. Then play Lick #3. End with Lick #1.

Solo #1

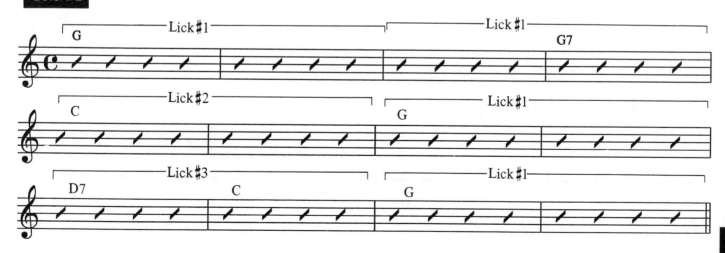

29

Lick #1

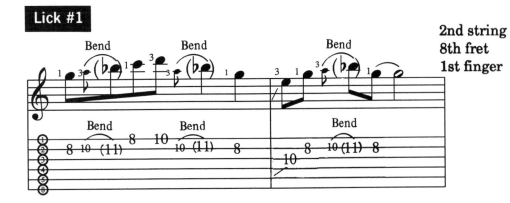

2nd string
8th fret
1st finger

Fingerboard position of left hand

Lick #2

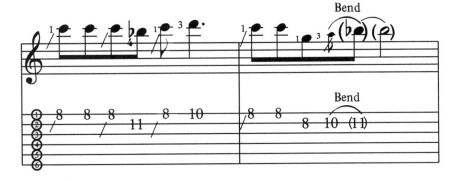

Lick #3

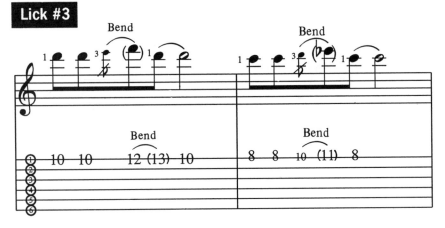

① Memorize the three licks.

② To play with the recording, play:
A. Lick #1 twice,
B. Lick #2 once,
C. Lick #1 once,
D. Lick #3 once,
E. Lick #1 once.

Solo #2

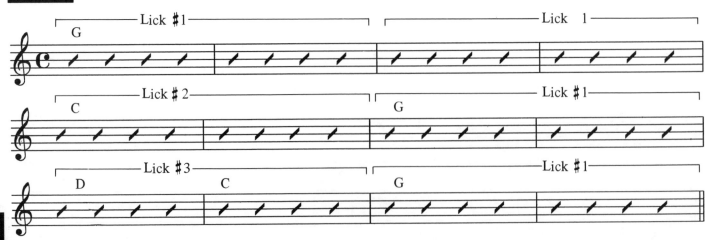

Lick #1

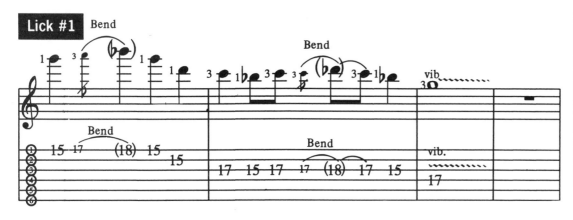

1st string
15th fret
1st finger

Lick #2

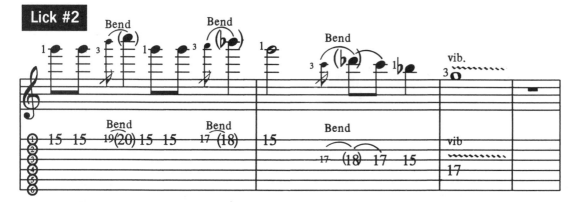

Lick #3

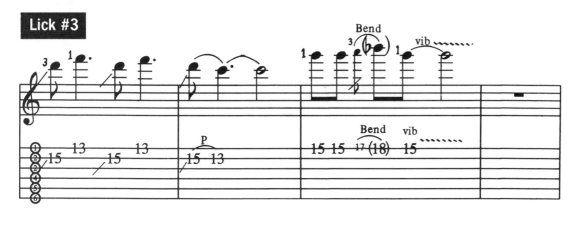

(1) Memorize Licks #1, #2, and #3.

(2) To play with the recording, play Lick #1, then Lick #2, then Lick #3.

Solo #3

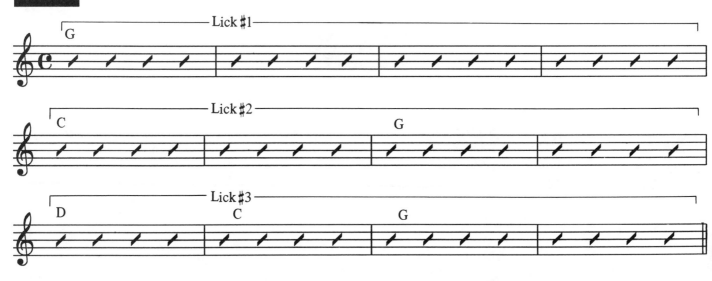

Reference Chord Table

G Major

Full Chords

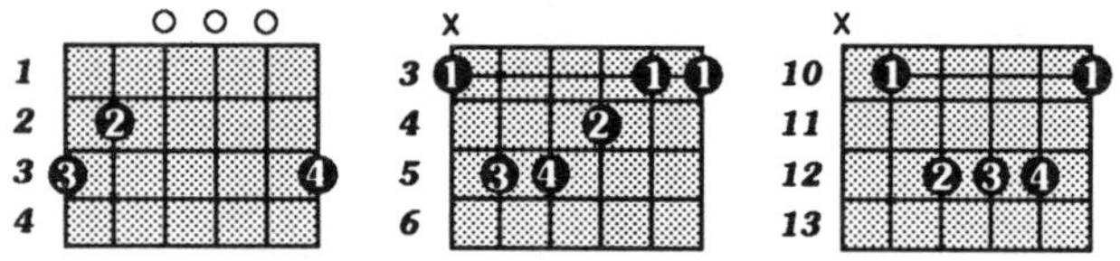

Power Chords

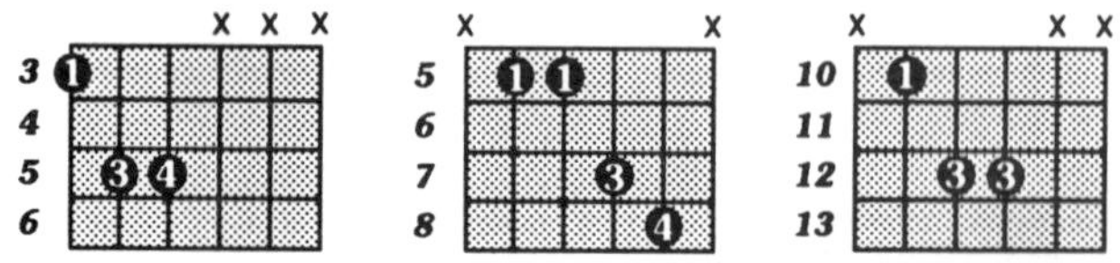

G7

Full Chords

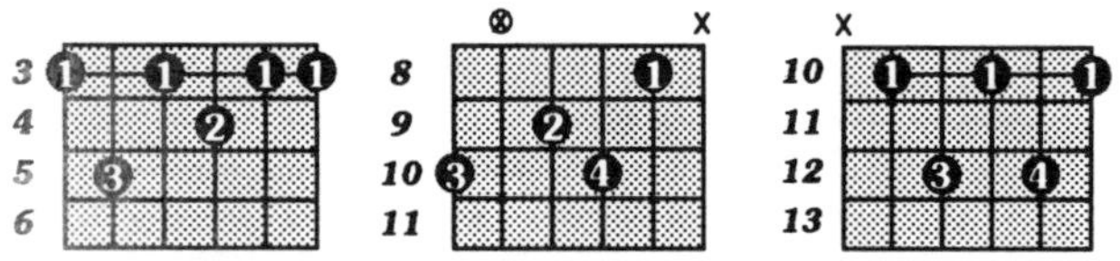

Power Chords

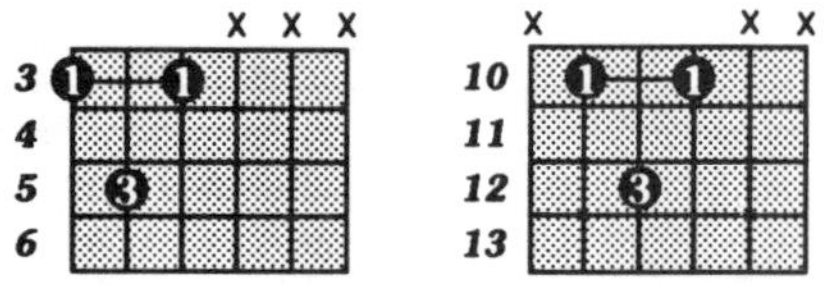

C

Full Chords

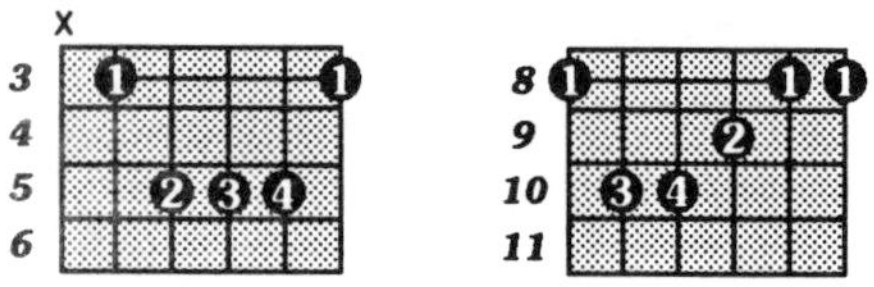

Power Chords

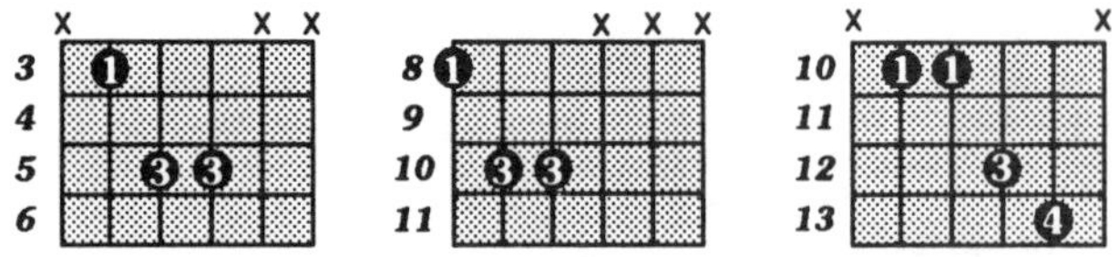

D7

Full Chords

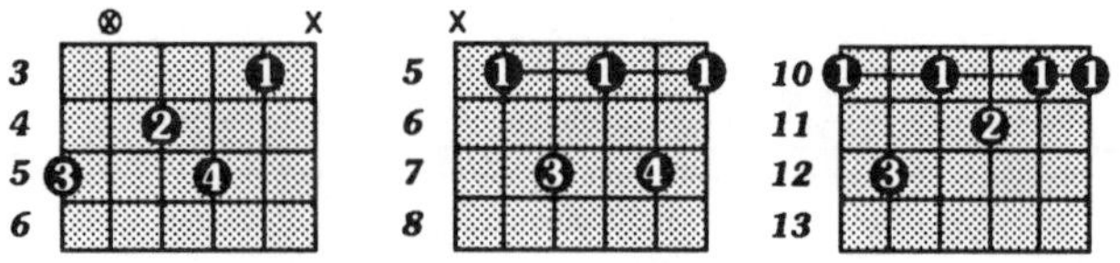

Power Chords

32

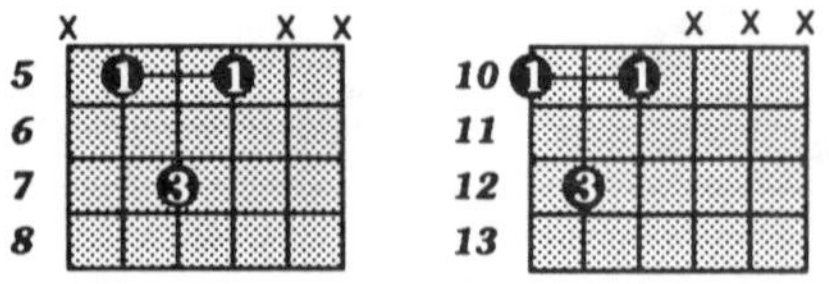

Basic Rhythm

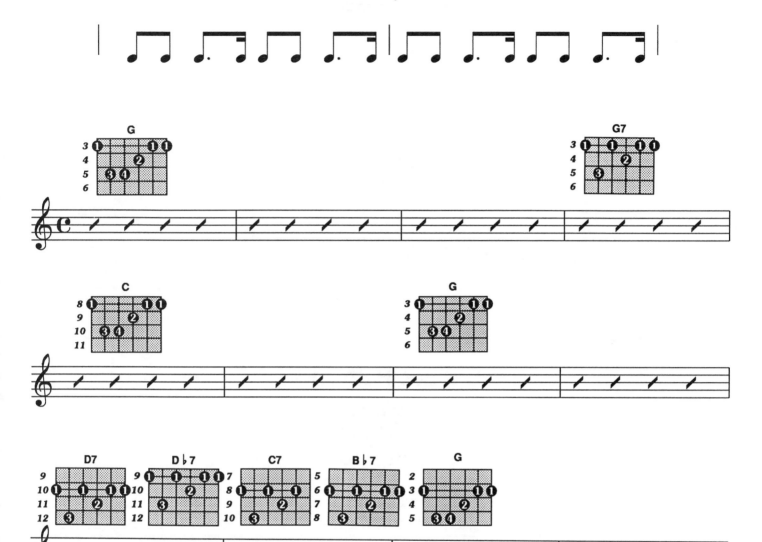

Now try the above using the following power chords:

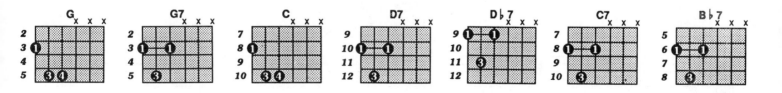

Basic Blues Runs

Practice all patterns going up and coming down.

G Blues Pattern #1

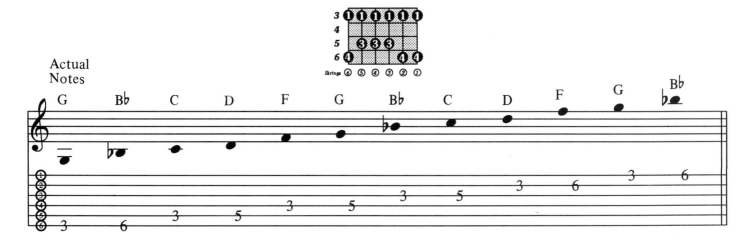

G Blues Pattern #2

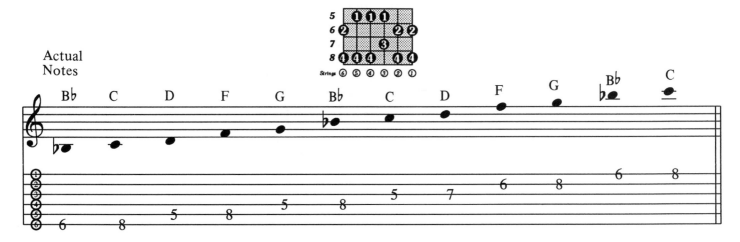

G Blues Pattern #3

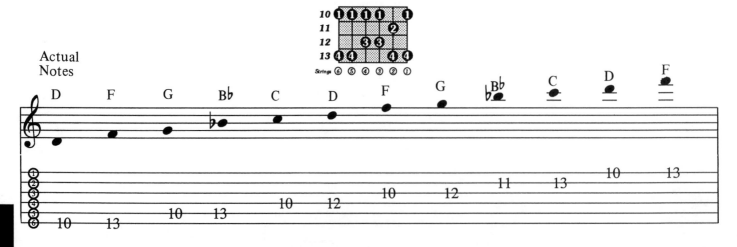

Driving Bass Solo / Key of D

Notes needed:

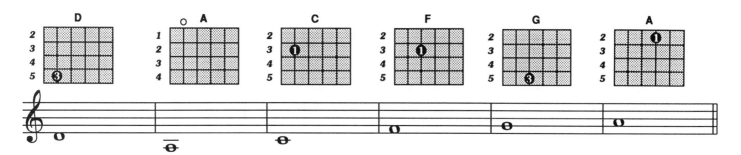

Drivin' D

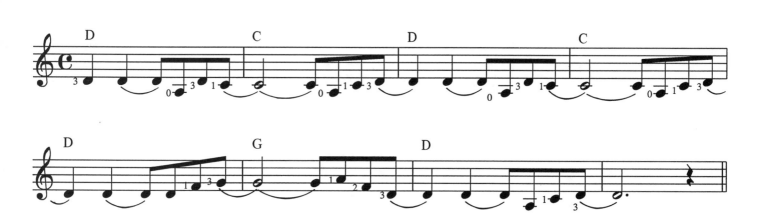

Lick #1

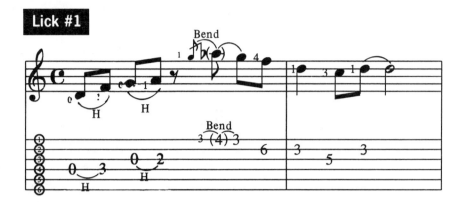

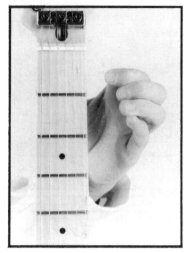

4th string / Open

Lick #2

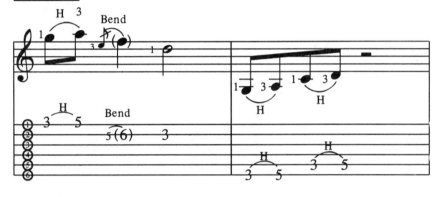

1. Memorize Licks #1, #2, and #3.
2. To play with the recording, play Lick #1 twice, then Lick #2, Lick #1, Lick #3, and end with Lick #1.

Lick #3

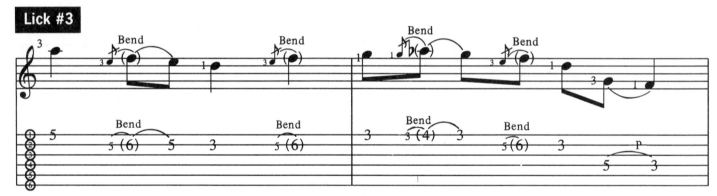

Solo #1

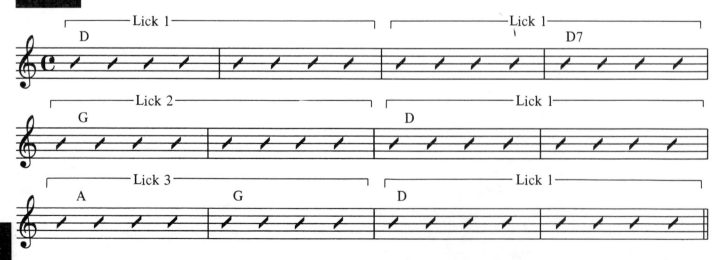

Lick #1

Lick #2

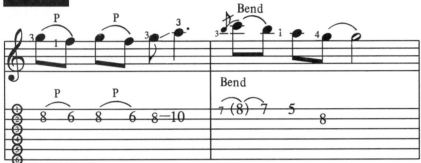

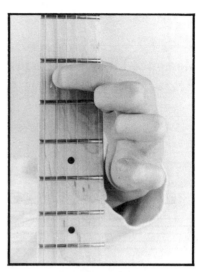

5th string
5th fret
1st finger

Lick #3

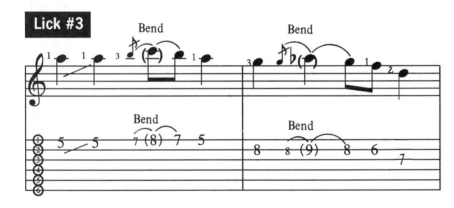

① Memorize Licks #1, #2, and #3.

② To play with the recording, play Lick #1 twice, then Lick #2, Lick #1, Lick #3, and end with Lick #1.

Solo #2

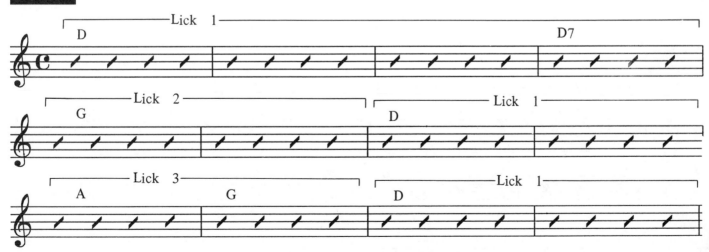

① Memorize Licks #1, #2, and #3.

② To play with the recording, play Lick #1, then Lick #2, and end with Lick #3.

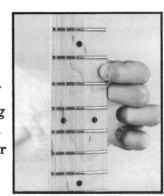

1st string
10th fret
1st finger

Lick #1

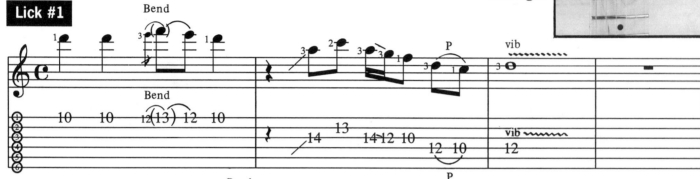

Lick #2

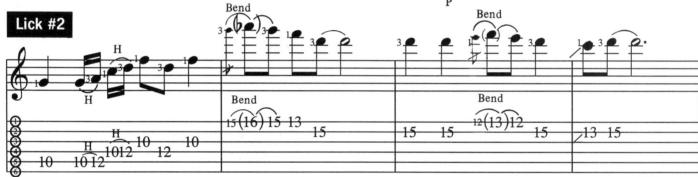

Lick #3

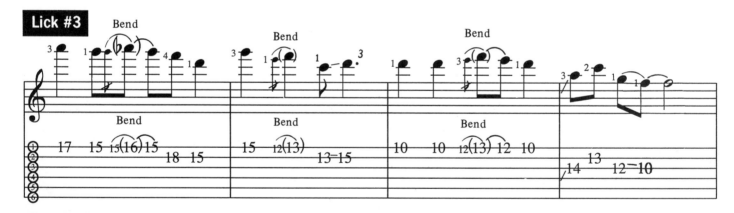

Solo #3

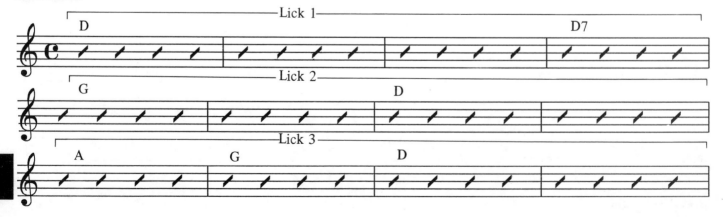

KEY OF D

Reference Chord Table

D Major

Full Chords   Power Chords

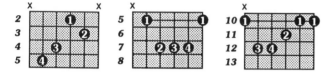

D7

Full Chords   Power Chords

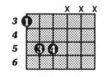
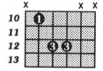

G

Full Chords   Power Chords

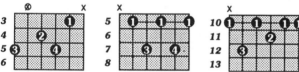
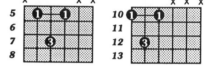

A7

Full Chords   Power Chords

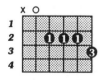
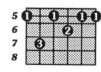
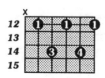
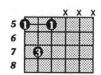
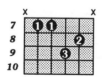
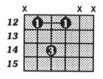

D CHORD STUDY #1

Basic Rhythm

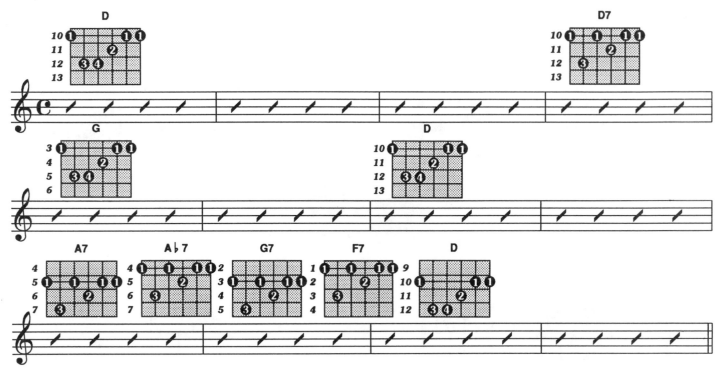

Now try the above using the following power chords:

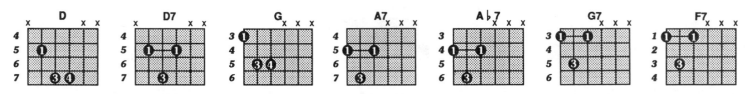

D CHORD STUDY #2

Pick each note of the following power chords individually.

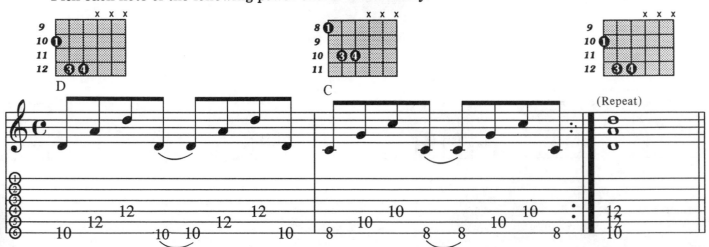

KEY OF D

Basic Blues Runs

Practice all patterns going up and coming down.

D Blues Pattern #1

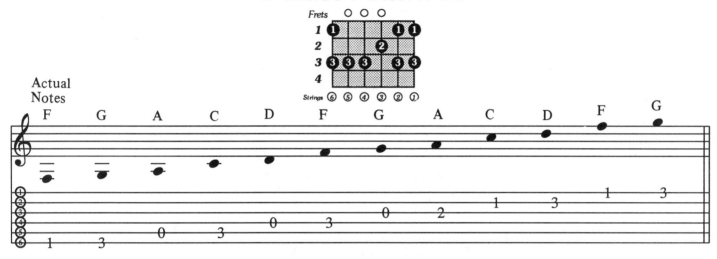

D Blues Pattern #2

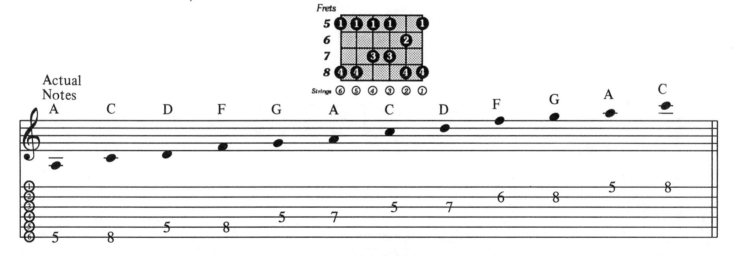

D Blues Pattern #3

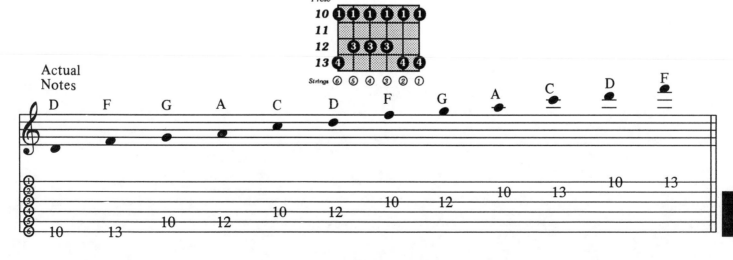

Driving Bass Solo / Key of A

Notes needed:

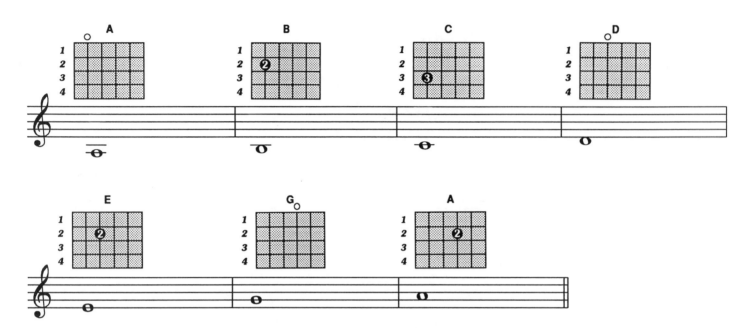

Do It!

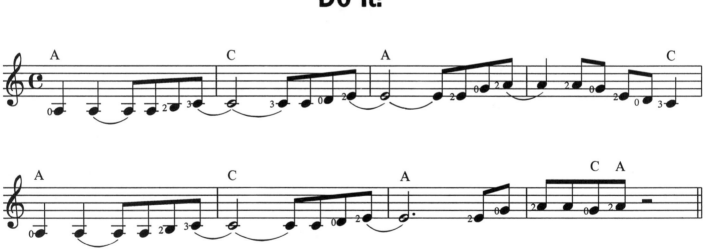

Lick #1

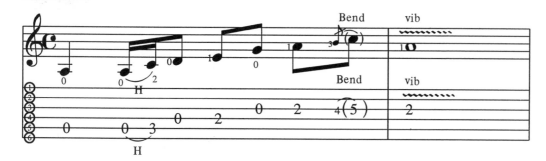

5th string /Open

Lick #2

Lick #3

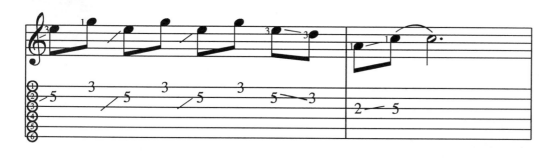

① Memorize Licks #1, #2, and #3.

② To play with the recording, play Lick #1 twice, then Lick #2. Go back to Lick #1. Next, play Lick #3. End with Lick #1.

Solo #1

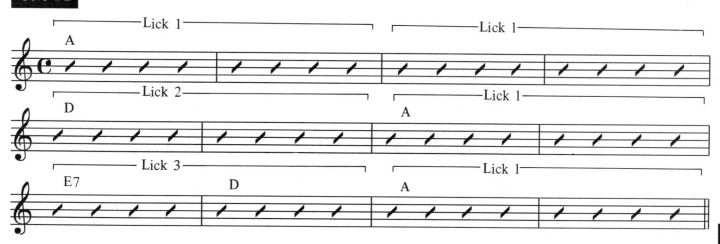

43

Lick #1

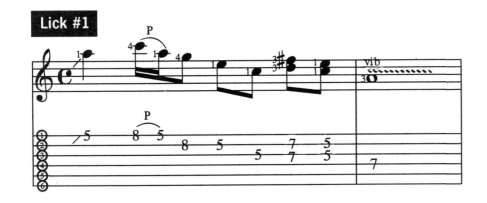

1st string
1st finger
5th fret

Lick #2

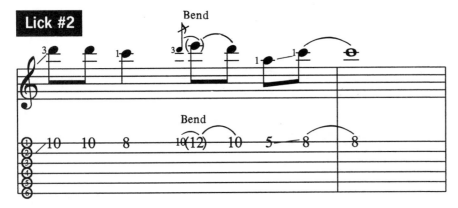

Lick #3

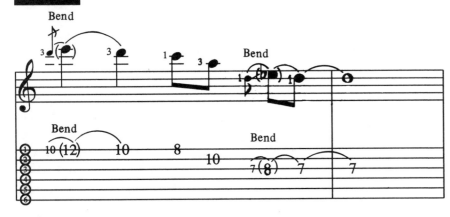

(1) Memorize Licks #1, #2, and #3.

(2) To play with the recording, play Lick #1 twice, then Lick #2. Play Lick #1 again. Next, play Lick #3. End with Lick #1.

Solo #2

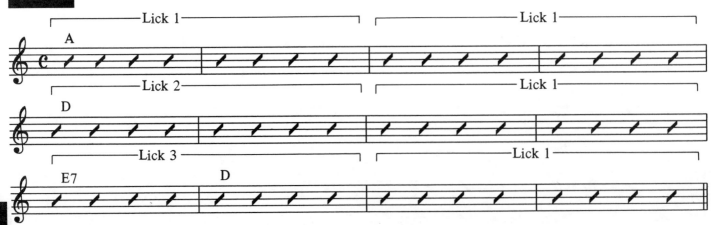

KEY-OF-A SOLO #3 / LICKS

1. Memorize Licks #1, #2, and #3.

2. To play with the recording, play Lick #1, then Lick #2, then Lick #3.

1st string
15th fret
3rd finger

Lick #1

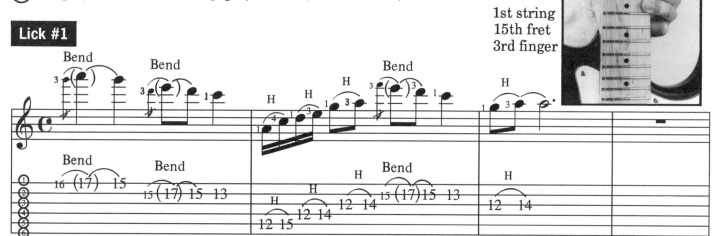

Lick #2

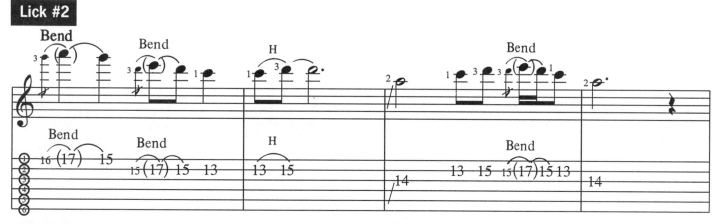

Lick #3

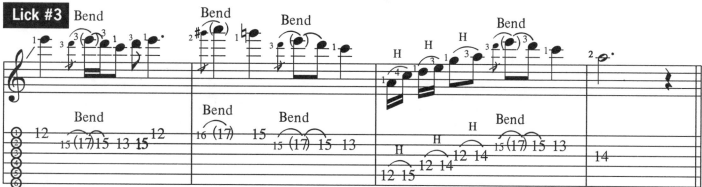

Solo #3

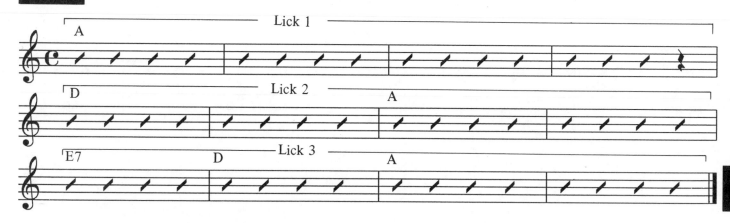

Reference Chord Table

A Major

Full Chords　　　　　　Power Chords

A7

Full Chords　　　　　　Power Chords

D

Full Chords　　　　　　Power Chords

E7

Full Chords　　　　　　Power Chords

46

Basic Rhythm

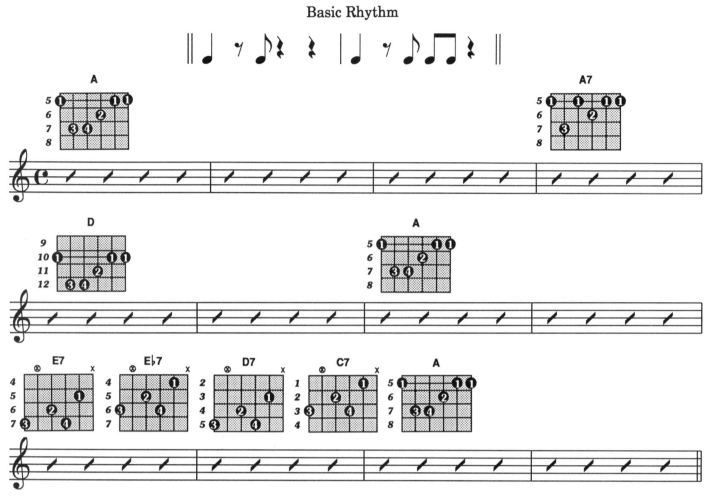

Now try the above using the following power chords:

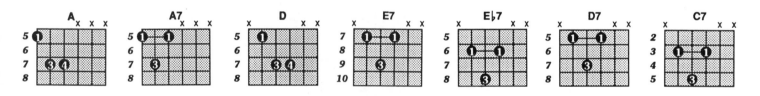

Power Riff

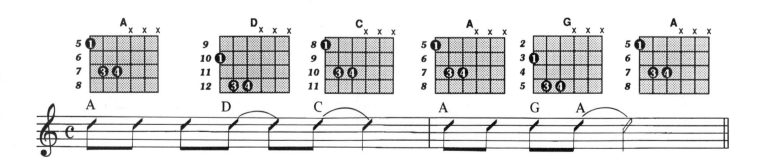

Basic Blues Runs

Practice all patterns going up and coming down.

A Blues Pattern #1

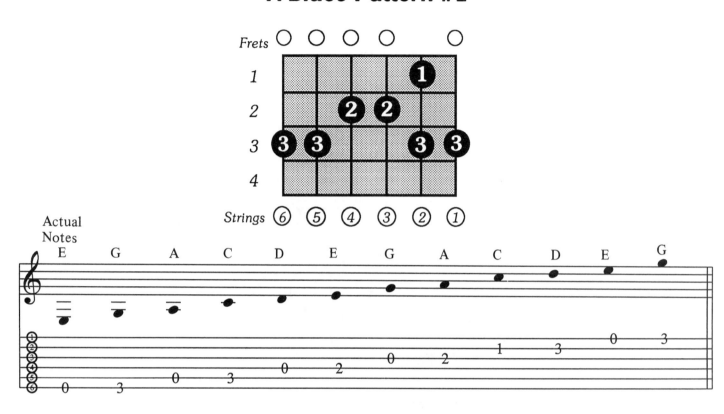

A Blues Pattern #2

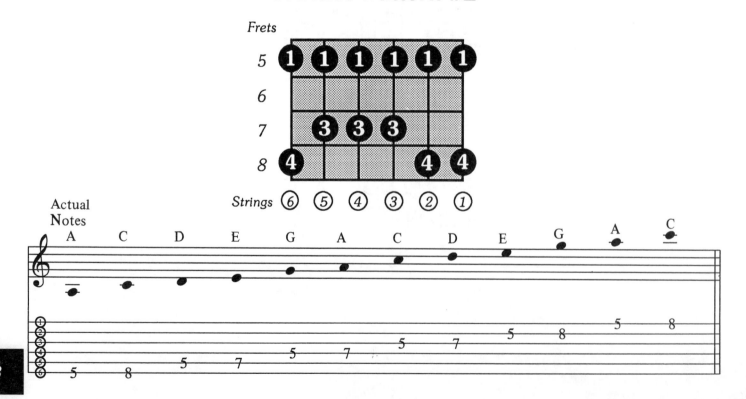

A Blues Pattern #3

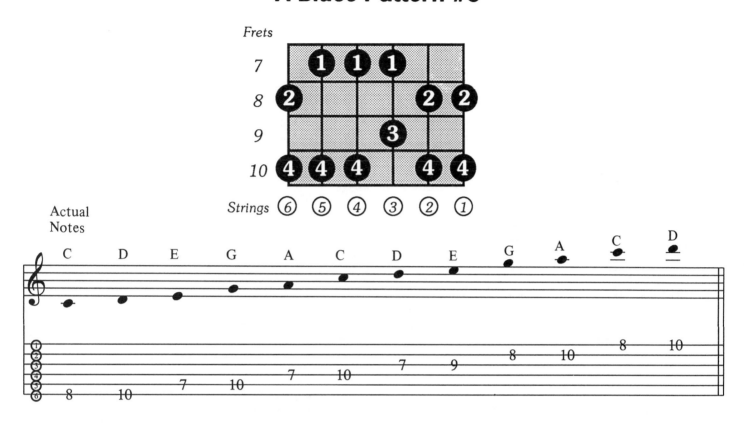

A Blues Pattern #4

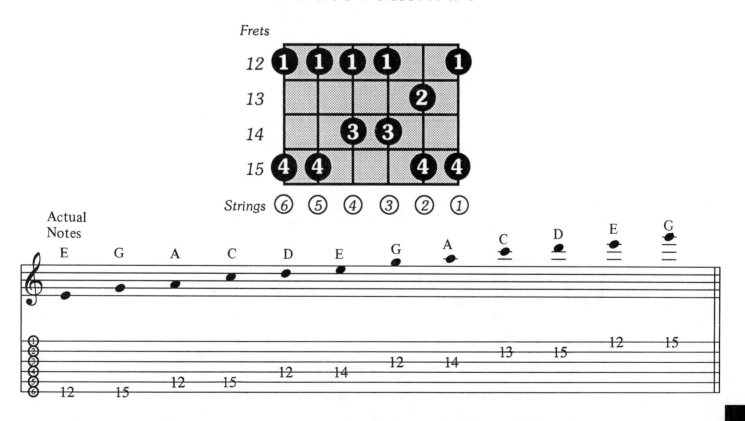

Driving Bass Solo / Key of C

Notes needed:

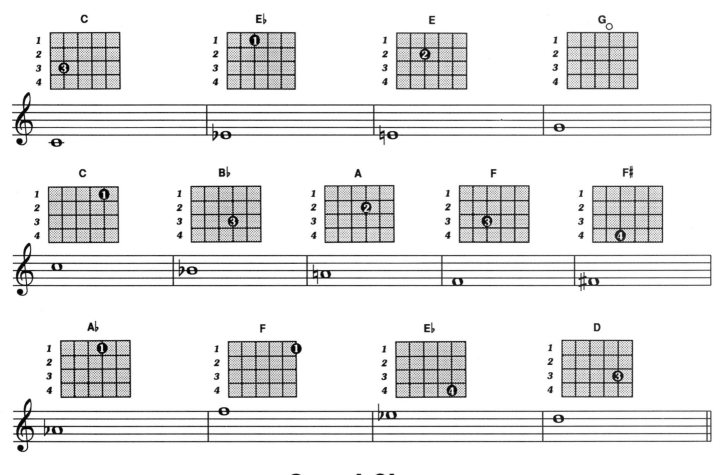

Grand Slam

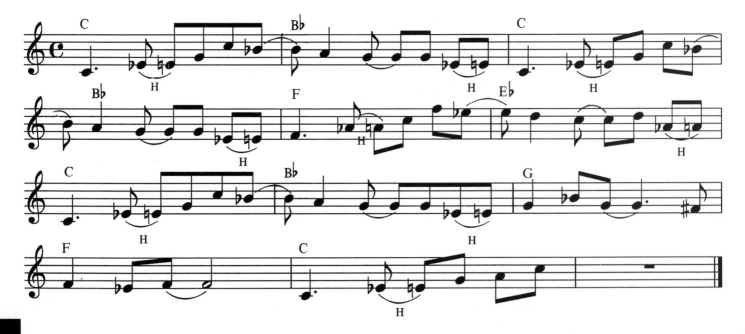

Lick #1

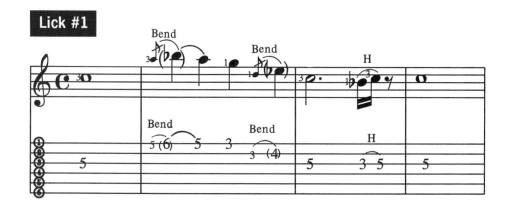

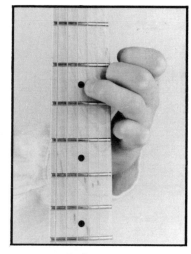

3rd string
5th fret
3rd finger

Lick #2

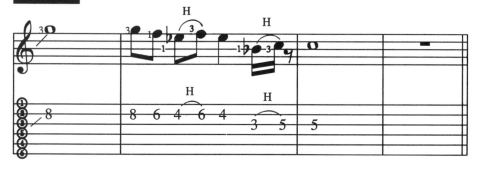

① Memorize Licks #1 and #2.

② To play with the recording, play Lick #1 twice, and then play Lick #2.

Solo #1

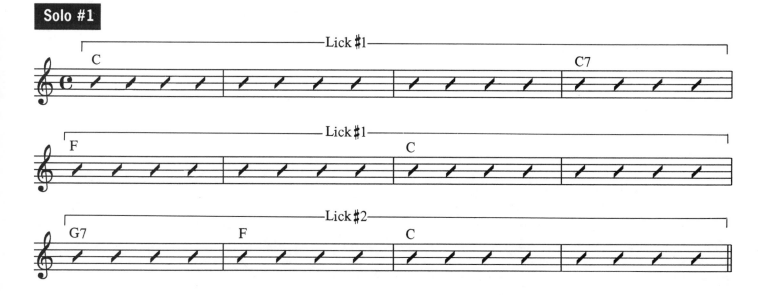

Lick #1

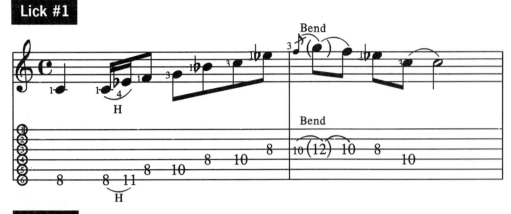

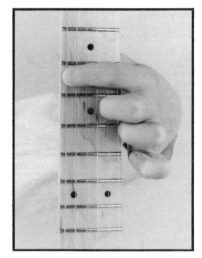

6th string
8th fret
1st finger

Lick #2

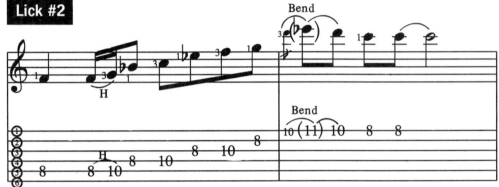

Lick #3

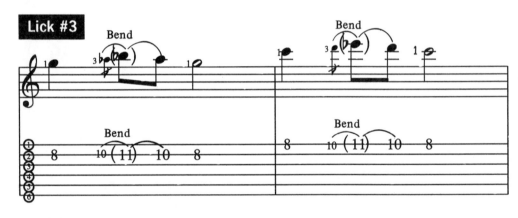

(1) Memorize Licks #1 and #2.

(2) To play with the recording, pla
Lick #1 twice, then play Lick #2
Play Lick #1 again. Next, play
Lick #3. End with Lick #1.

Solo #2

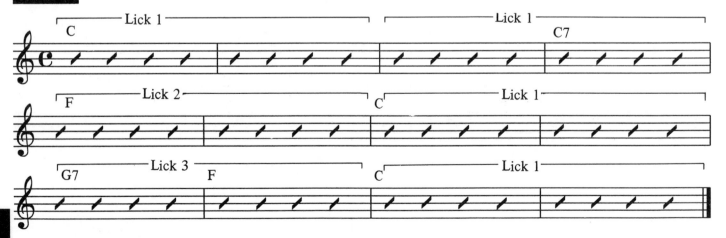

Lick #1

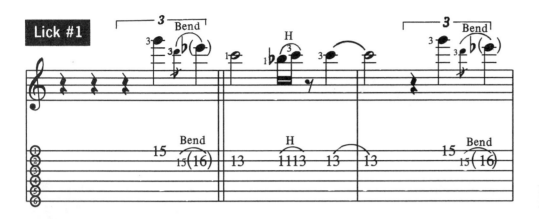

1st string
15th fret
3rd finger

Lick #2

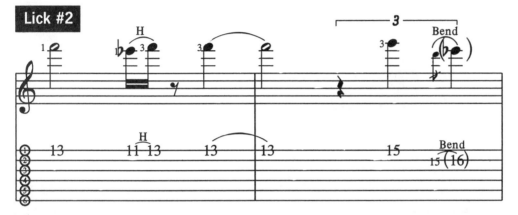

Lick #3

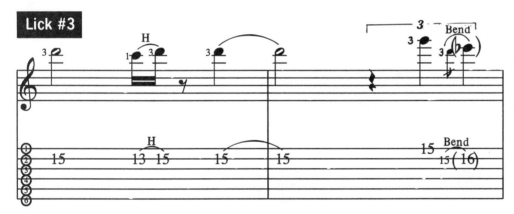

1. Memorize Licks #1, #2, and #3.

2. To play with the recording, play Lick #1 twice, then play Lick #2. Next, play Lick #1 again. Play Lick #3. End with Lick #1.

Solo #3

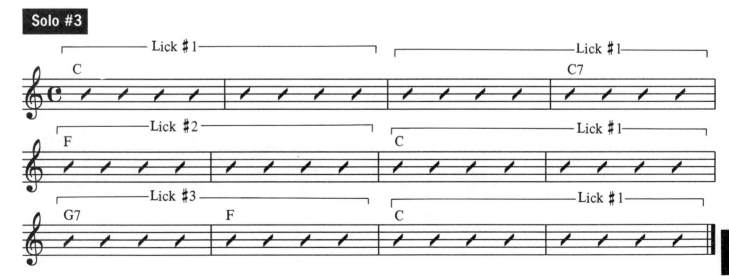

Reference Chord Table

C Major

Full Chords   Power Chords

C7

Full Chords   Power Chords

F

Full Chords   Power Chords

G7

Full Chords   Power Chords

Basic Rhythm

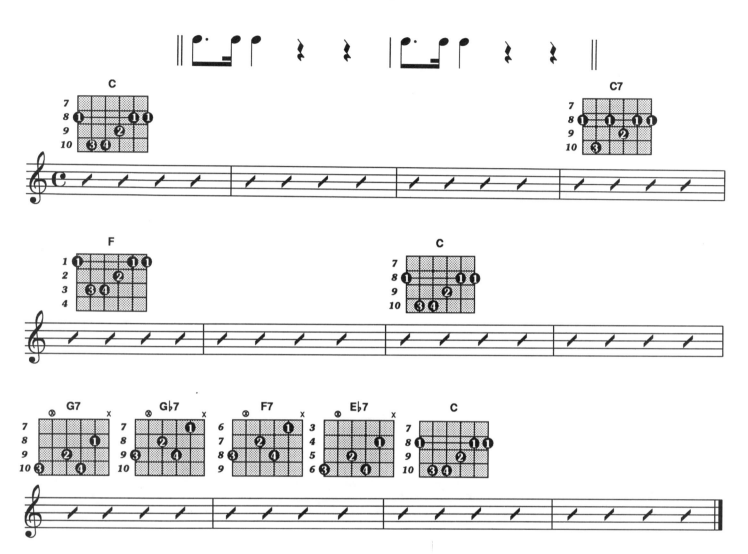

Now try the above using the following power chords:

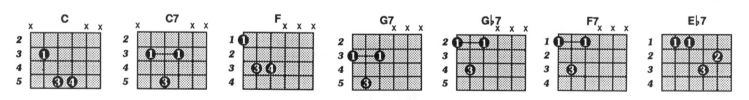

Rhythm Break

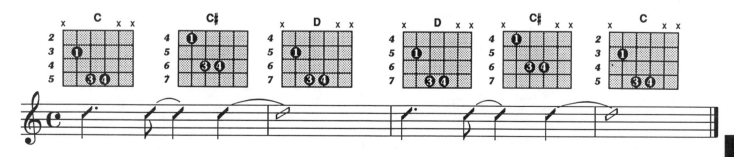

Basic Blues Runs

Practice all patterns going up and coming down.

C Blues Pattern #1

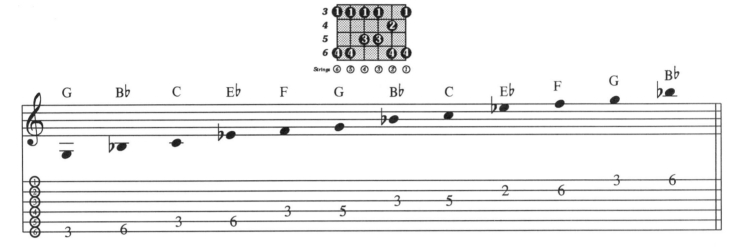

C Blues Pattern #2

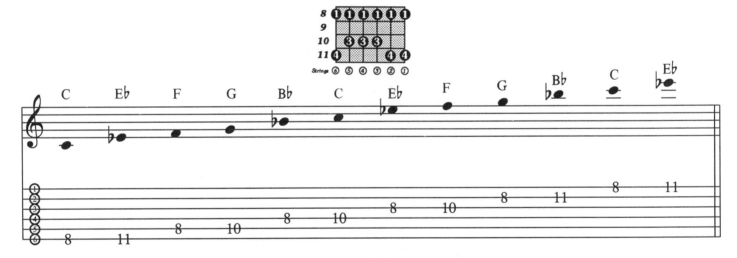

C Blues Pattern #3

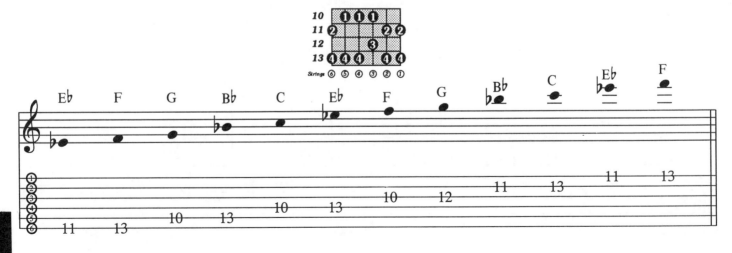

Driving Bass Solo / Key of F

Notes needed:

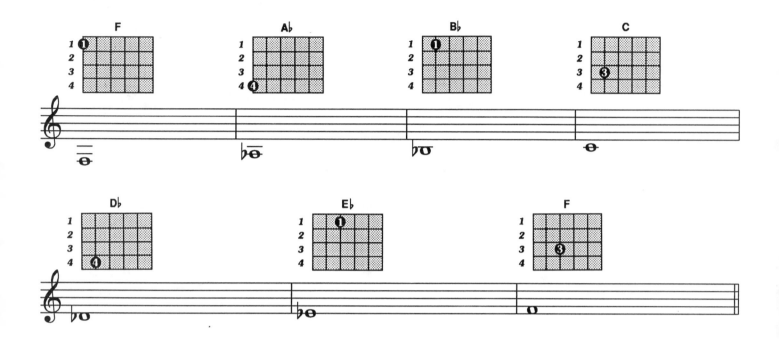

Down Shift

(1) Memorize Licks #1, #2, and #3.

(2) To play with the recording, play Lick #1 twice, then play Lick #2.
Play Lick #1 again. End with Lick #3.

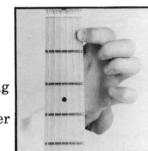

1st string
1st fret
1st finger

Lick #1

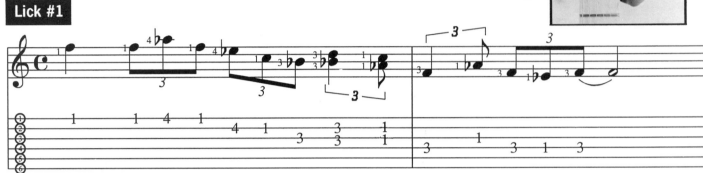

Lick #2

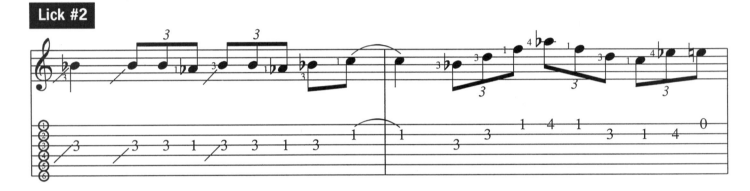

Lick #3

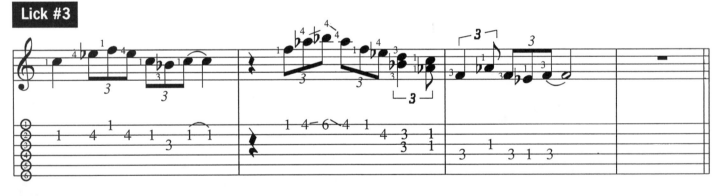

Solo #1

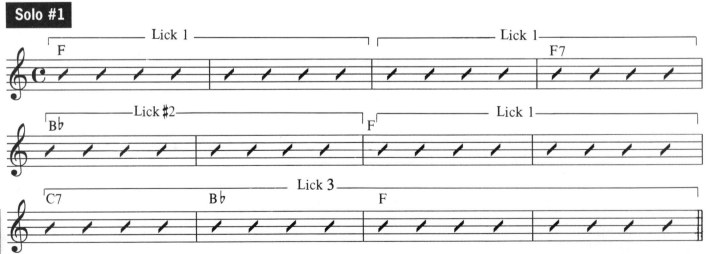

KEY-OF-F SOLO #2 / LICKS

① Memorize Licks #1, #2, and #3.

② To play with the recording, play Lick #1 twice, then play Lick #2. Play Lick #1 again, and then Lick #3. End with Lick #1.

2nd string
6th fret
1st finger

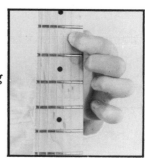

Lick #1

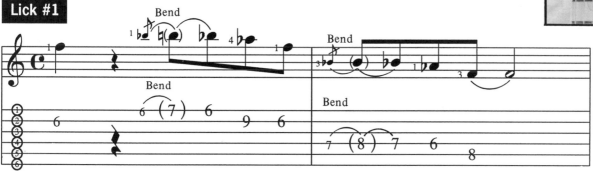

Lick #2

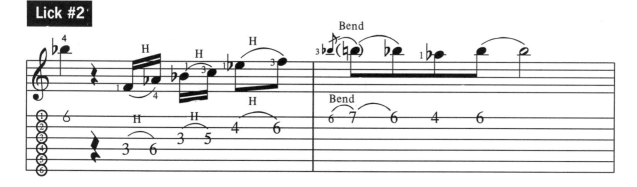

Lick #3

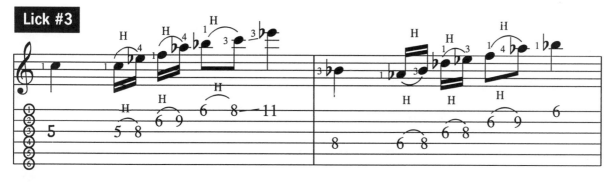

Solo #2

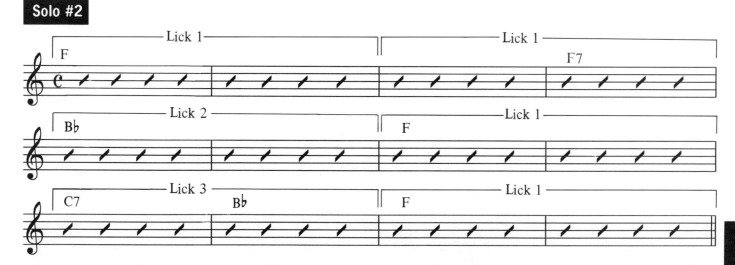

① Memorize Licks #1, #2, and #3.
② To play with the recording, play Lick #1 twice, then play Lick #2.
　　　Repeat Lick #1. Play Lick #3 and end with Lick #1.

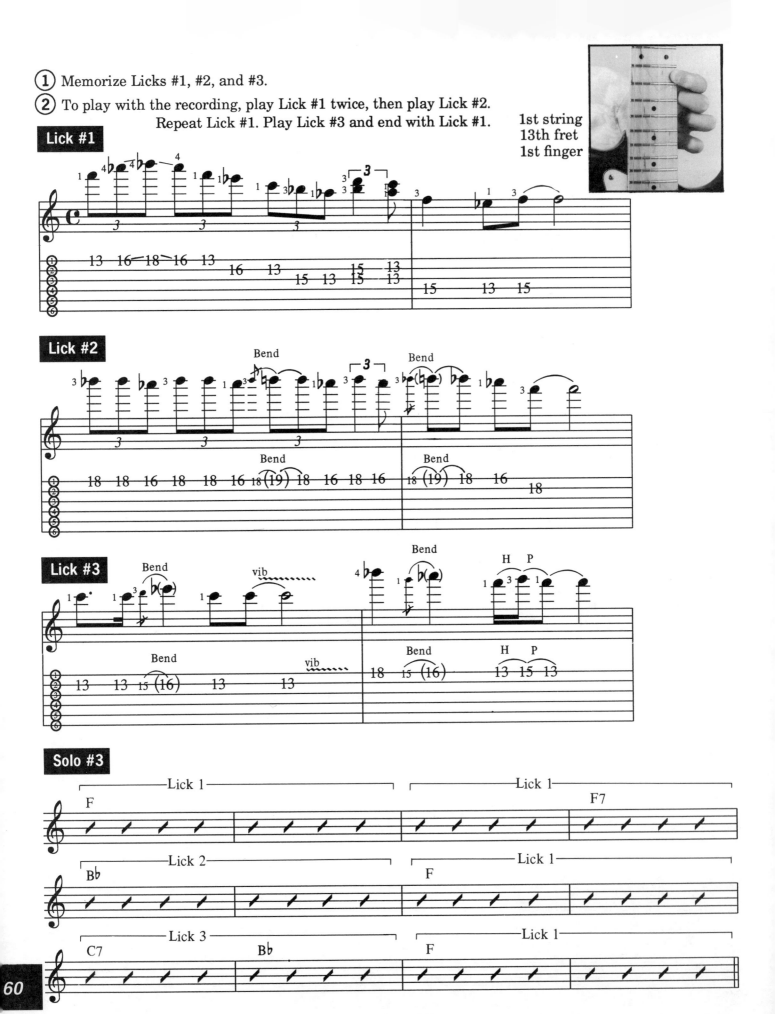

KEY OF F

Reference Chord Table

F Major

Full Chords   Power Chords

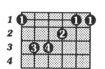 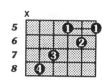 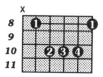

F7

Full Chords   Power Chords

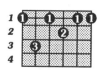 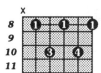

B♭

Full Chords   Power Chords

 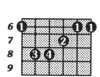   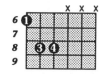 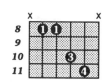

C7

Full Chords   Power Chords

  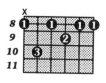   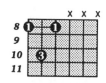 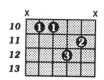

Basic Rhythm

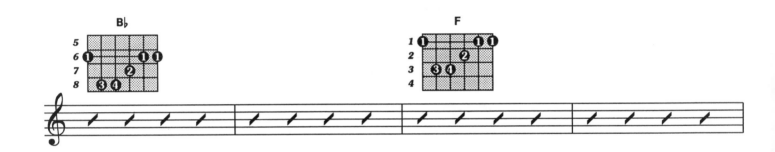

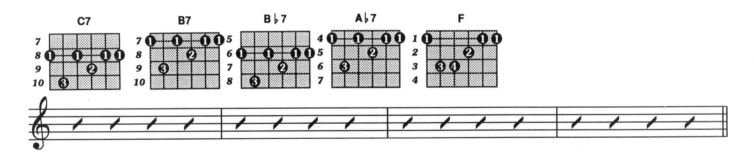

Now try the above using the following power chords:

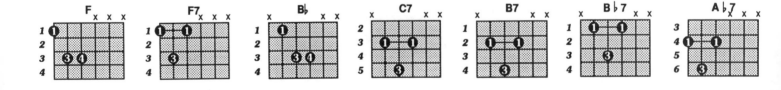

"Fill-In" Rhythm

Frequently, when playing rock and blues rhythm, you can add much to the piece by adding a short blues run between rhythm phrases. Here is an example of how this works:

Basic Blues Runs

Practice all patterns going up and coming down.

F Blues
Pattern #1

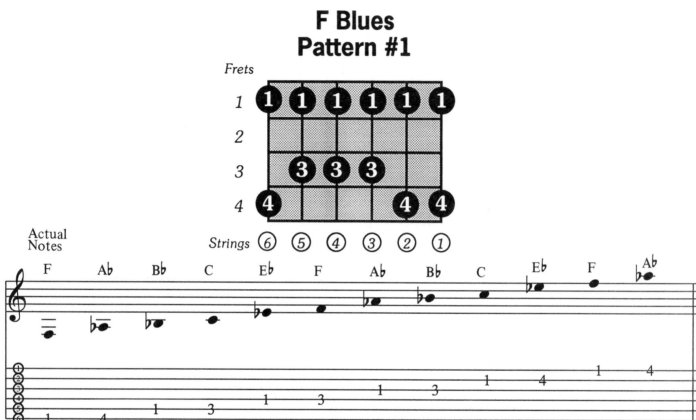

F Blues
Pattern #2

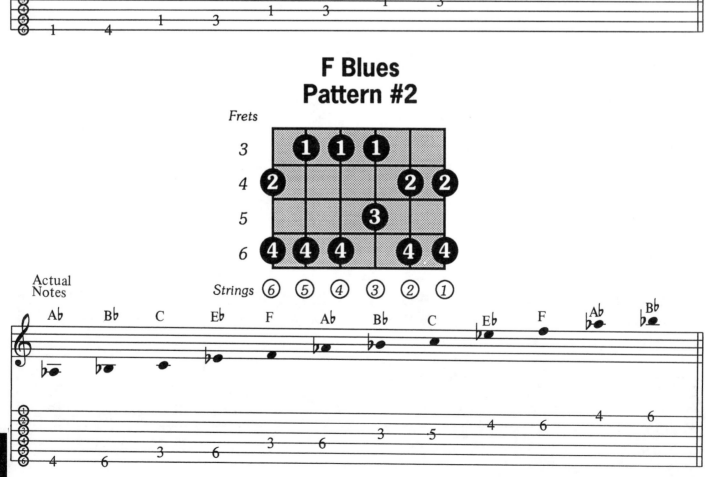

F Blues
Pattern #3

F Blues
Pattern #4*

*You will notice that *F Blues Pattern #4* is exactly like *F Blues Pattern #1,* only it is 12 frets higher!

Driving Bass Solo / Key of B♭

Notes needed:

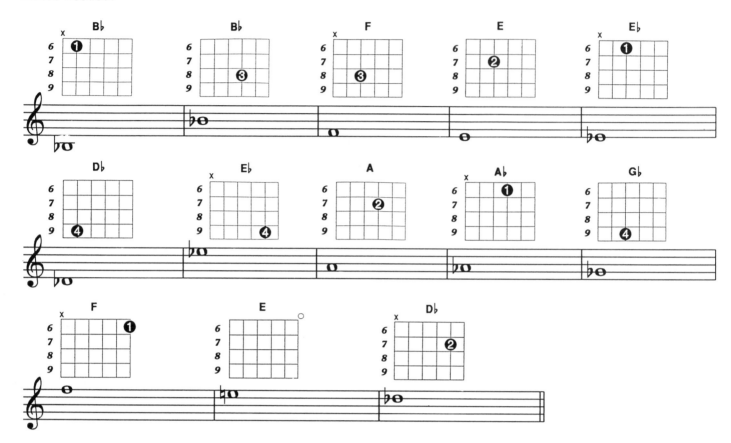

Funk Drive

KEY-OF-B♭ SOLO #1 / LICKS

(1) Memorize Licks #1, #2, and #3.

(2) To play with the recording, play Lick #1 twice, then play Lick #2. Play Lick #1 again, and then Lick #3. End on Lick #1.

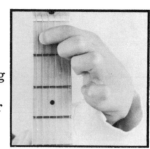

5th string
1st fret
1st finger

Lick #1

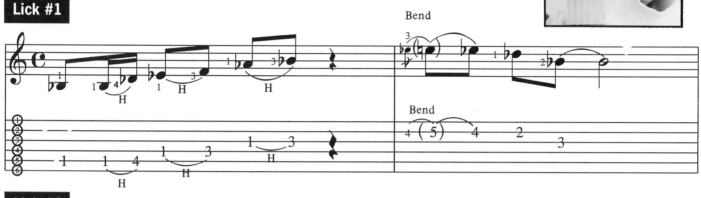

Lick #2

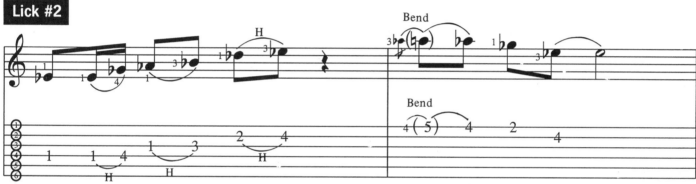

Lick #3

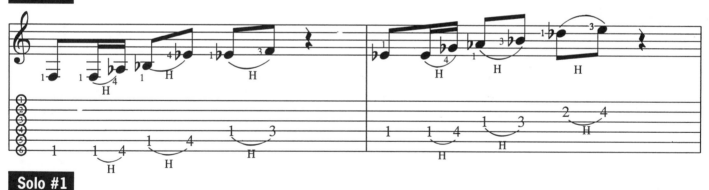

Solo #1

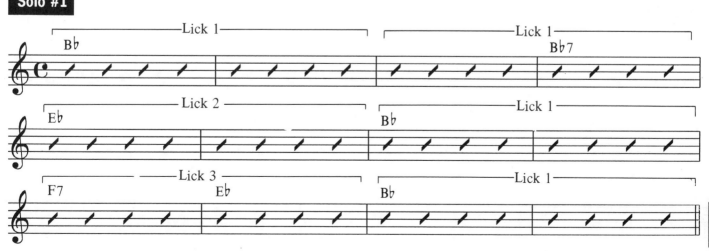

Lick #1

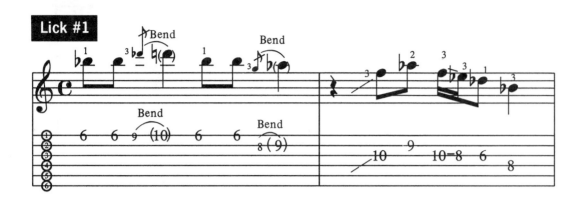

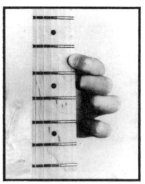

1st string
6th fret
1st finger

Lick #2

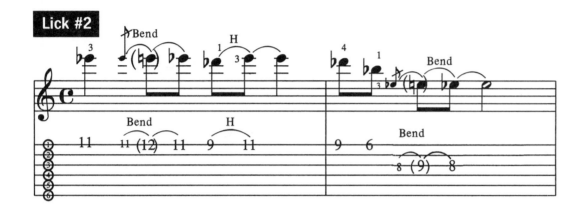

Lick #3

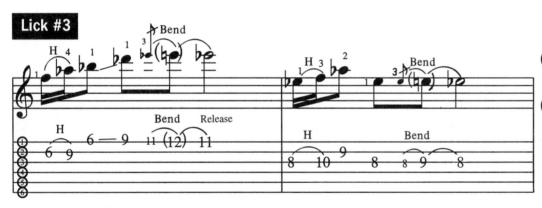

(1) Memorize Licks #1, #2, and #3.

(2) To play with the recording, play Lick #1 twice, then play Lick #2. Play Lick #1 again, and then Lick #3. End on Lick #1.

Solo #2

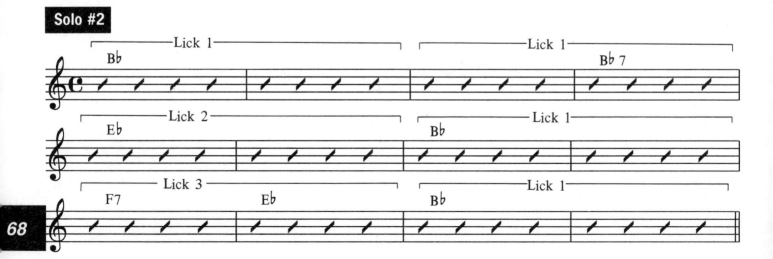

3rd string
15th fret
3rd finger

Lick #1

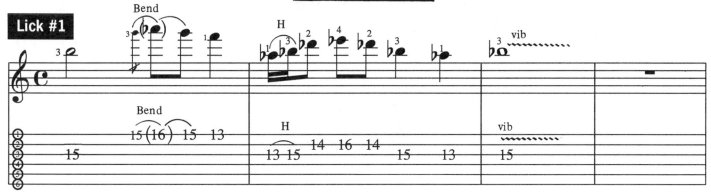

Lick #2

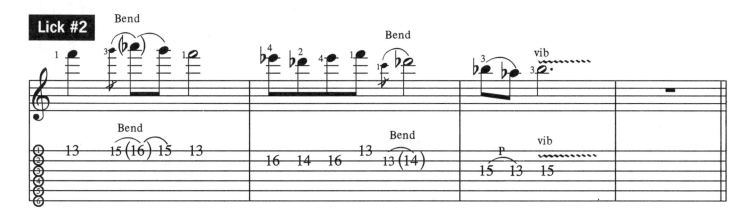

① Memorize Licks #1 and #2.

② To play with the recording, play Lick #1 twice, then play Lick #2.

Solo #3

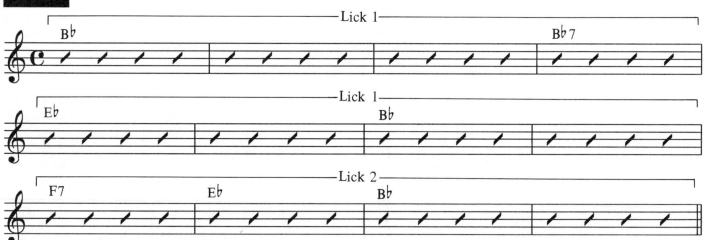

Reference Chord Table

B♭ Major

Full Chords   Power Chords

B♭7

Full Chords   Power Chords

E♭

Full Chords   Power Chords

F7

Full Chords   Power Chords

Basic Rhythm

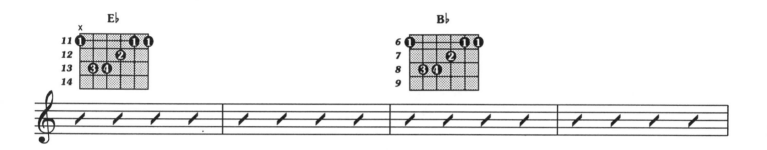

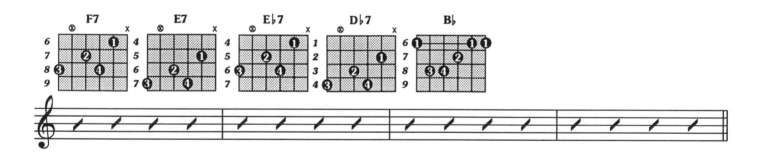

Now try the above using the following power chords:

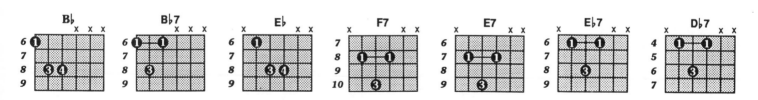

Basic Blues Runs

Practice all patterns going up and coming down.

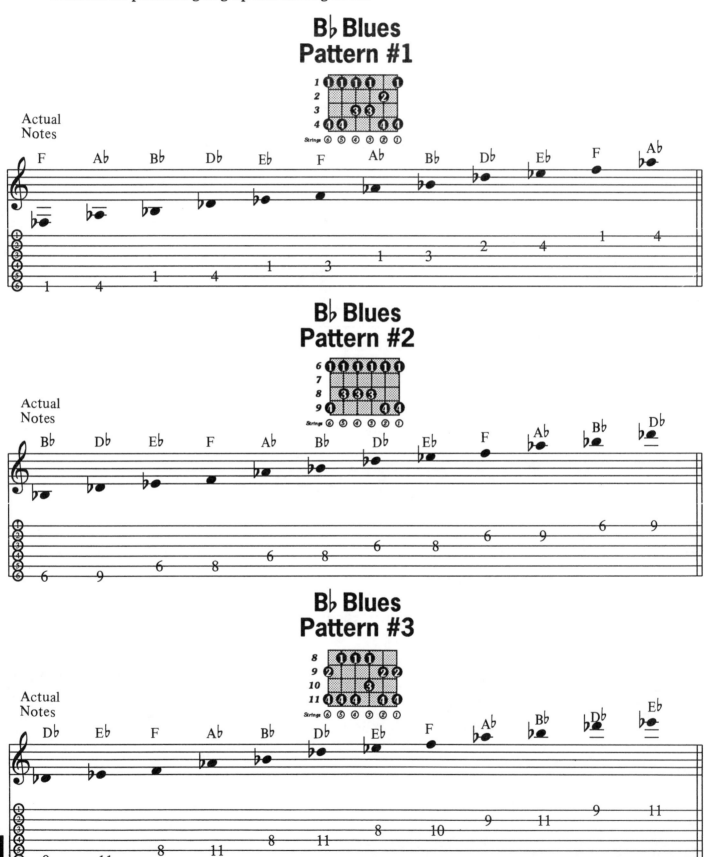

SECTION TWO/

ROCK GUITAR HANDBOOK

BY MARK LONERGAN

First, Some Basics . . .

One evening in 1971, a New Jersey music store owner taught me the three most important things that any budding rock guitarist can learn: 1) the barre chord, 2) the pentatonic scale, and 3) the "bent string." Together with 4) the hammer-on and the pull-off, they provide the basis for just about *every* rock guitar style.

1) *The barre chord* is so named because *one* finger is used to "barre" several strings at once. The basis for virtually every rock rhythm guitar pattern from Chuck Berry to Eddie Van Halen, the barre chord uses no open strings and is therefore "movable"—a rhythm pattern using barre chords in the key of G (at the 3rd fret) can be transposed instantly to the key of A simply by moving the entire pattern to the *5th* fret. Here are the basic positions:

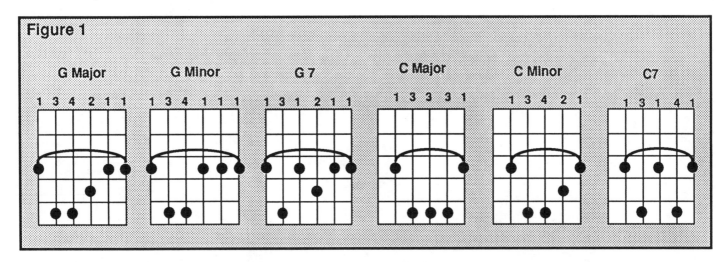

Figure 1

G Major   G Minor   G 7   C Major   C Minor   C7

All fingerings are in the 3rd position. If you are completely new to this, you may find these chords awkward (*I* certainly did, if that's any consolation); but, with patience and practice, you will soon find them becoming quite easy to play. For many modern styles, you may find it desirable to play only the three lowest notes of the standard barre chords—technically, an octave with a perfect 5th inner voice and, unofficially, a power chord. Here are the three basic fingerings given in the 3rd position. They are designated as G5, C5, and F5 forms:

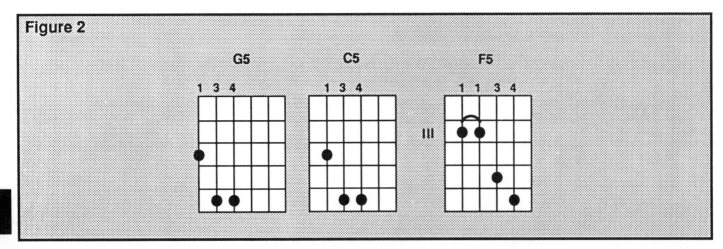

Figure 2

G5   C5   F5

2) *The pentatonic scale* is a five-note scale that is probably the basis for more rock and blues solos than any five other scales combined. For our purposes, we will deal primarily with the *minor* pentatonic scale, which appears in many patterns on the fingerboard, undoubtedly the most important of which is the one in Figure 3.

This useful pattern is known as "the box position" obviously because the diagram showing its fingering looks somewhat like a box. As unassuming as it may look, however, this pattern is "home base" for an

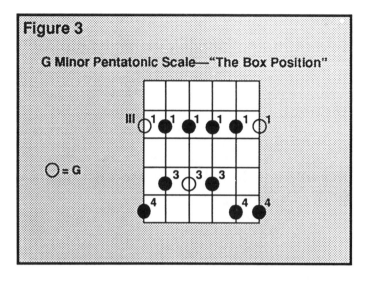

Figure 3

G Minor Pentatonic Scale—"The Box Position"

overwhelming majority of rock solos from the most basic to the most advanced. While many fine guitarists from Arlen Roth to Eddie Van Halen suggest playing the notes at the 6th fret with the ring finger of the left hand (because of its strength), I'm more comfortable using my pinky in normal circumstances and reaching up to the 6th fret with my ring finger only to bend strings (but more on that later). Like the barre chord, the box position is movable—in fact, it moves with the barre chord. The G box position is located at the 3rd fret, the A box position at the 5th, and so on.

3) *The bent string* is the wail, the cry characteristic of all blues-based music—and, therefore, of all rock guitar playing. Example 1 shows the proper technique for bending—place *as many fingers as possible* (usually three, but in many instances two will do) on the string and use them *all* to push it until it literally bends and the tone of the note you are playing becomes correspondingly higher. The number below the grace note (the tiny note with the line through its stem) indicates the fret *played*, while the number in parentheses indicates the fret at which the sound *to which you are bending* is located. I realize that sounds confusing, but take a look at Example 1:

Example 1

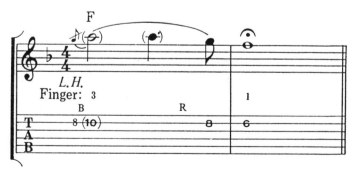

All you have to do to play it is smack three fingers down on the B string at the *8th* fret, pick the note, then bend the string until you hear the same sound as the one that appears naturally at the *10th* fret. It may take some time and practice before you're able to hit the note right on the button every time or to hold it steady for a long period, but it is really much easier than it might seem at first. Also, try experimenting with finger vibrato—rocking the string just slightly back and forth for a quavering, emotional sound. You'll hear this effect frequently on the accompanying cassette and in just about any rock guitar solo.

4) Examples 2 and 3 illustrate two related slurring techniques, the *hammer-on* and the *pull-off*, which help produce a smoother, more fluid sound and increase speed. To hammer on, pick the first note on a given string, then quickly strike the next note with sufficient force to make it ring *without* using your pick:

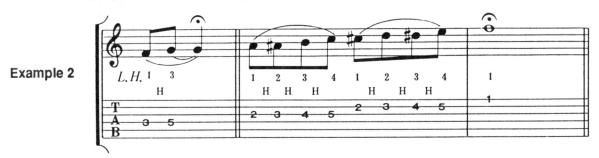

Example 2

The pull-off is pretty much the reverse of the hammer. Pick the first note, then quickly pull the fingertip from the string with sufficient force to cause the next lower note to ring:

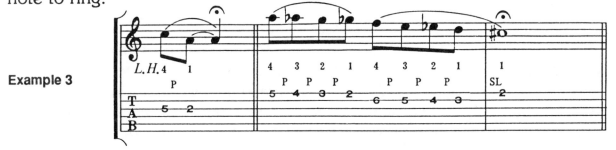

Example 3

Most rock guitarists seem to favor hammers and pull-offs over the alternative of picking every note (the technique preferred by many jazz players), and many of the licks included in this section of the book are designed to be played using hammers and pull-offs almost exclusively. But it's important to remember that, whatever the technique, playing smoothly and evenly is necessary. Even when playing a torrent of slurred notes, don't lose track of the beat and its subdivisions or your solos will sound chaotic.

Testing the Water

Examples 4 and 5 are four-bar phrases based on typical motifs heard in the playing of just about every rock guitarist from Jimi Hendrix and Eric Clapton to Prince and Mark Knopfler (which is not really such a leap when you think about it, but you know what I mean).

Example 4 relies heavily on a rapidly repeated series of pull-offs and hammer-ons based on the G minor pentatonic scale to create tension before resolving to the final B natural, which suggests a G major or G7 chord. Be sure to follow the left-hand fingering instructions immediately below the standard musical notation.

Example 4

Also based on the G minor pentatonic "box position," Example 5 should prove relatively easy if you follow the picking directions above the staff. The mark that looks like a staple indicates a *downstroke*, while the "V" predictably calls for an *upstroke*. Other players have different opinions on the subject of pick direction, but I've found standard up/down alternating picking works best most of the time.

Example 5

And, Finally . . .

Now let's *really* start playing. Example 6 is a typical rhythm guitar part built entirely around the barre chord forms shown earlier. We're playing in the key of C here, so the pattern begins at the 8th fret—8th position.

To play it, strike only the two lowest notes of the standard barre chord forms, use downstrokes only, and *muffle* or *damp* the strings just slightly with the heel of your right hand for a more percussive, thumpy sound. The arrowheads below the first downbeat and second upbeat of each measure are there to tell you to *accent* those beats by hitting the notes with a bit more force and easing up on the damping effect just a little. By the way, the accent pattern created this way is based on the Charleston beat that was so popular in the early years of this century; so the next time someone tells you about "New Music . . . ."

Example 6

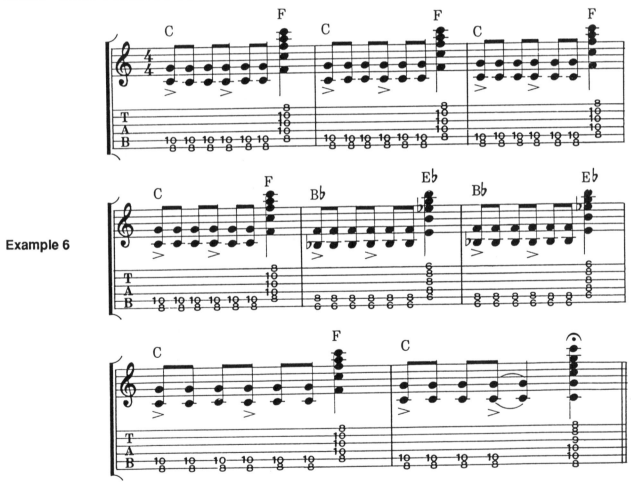

Sounds sort of like something you might hear on an early Cars record, doesn't it? (At least I *hope* it does. . . .) Anyway, now that you've played the rhythm part, here are two solos based on the box position at the 8th fret and designed to highlight the techniques we've discussed so far. They're not too difficult, but you may want to try playing them more slowly than the recorded version on the accompanying cassette; so why not rewind the tape to the beginning of the rhythm part (Example 6) and practice Examples 7 and 8 along with it.

Example 7

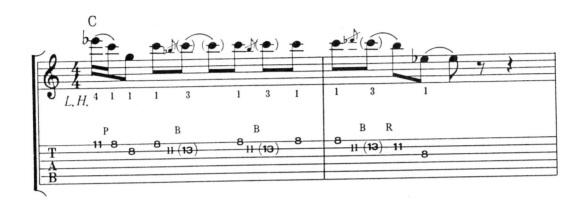

Example 8

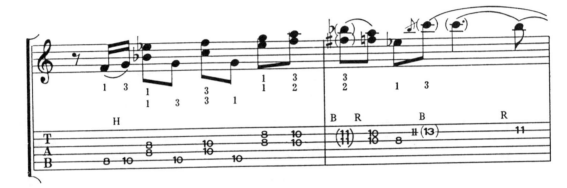

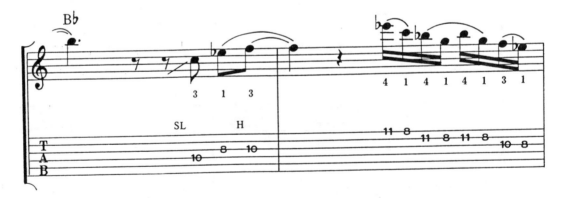

... And Here's Another Useful Technique

The trill is really nothing more than a series of repeated, very fast pull-offs and hammer-ons. An exciting, tension-building effect, the trill is heard frequently in the playing of Jeff Beck, Jimi Hendrix, and Prince, and is especially powerful when combined with bending or whammy-bar techniques or electronic devices such as the wah-wah pedal.

To strengthen the fingers of the left hand for the trill, try anchoring the index finger at the 5th fret of the high E string and slowly but evenly—be sure to use a metronome—play a succession of sixteenth-note pull-offs and hammer-ons first using the pinky, then the ring finger, and finally the middle finger. Initially, you will find your fingers tiring quickly; but, as you practice, the technique will become second nature. Gradually build up speed by moving the metronome up a notch at a time.

Example 9

The First Guitar Hero

Although the ingredients that came together to form rock and roll date back at least a century, and although its rise has taken it around the world and through countless changes, one fact remains as true today as it was 30 years ago when rock was in its infancy: The most influential instrumentalist in rock and roll remains the guitarist-singer-songwriter whose style virtually *defined* rock and roll, whose solos provided the common vocabulary for all the rockers who followed him, and whose songs may just represent the pinnacle of America's contribution to international culture. But don't get me wrong—the main reason for Chuck Berry's popularity among both guitarists and the public in general is that his music is so much fun to listen to—and so much fun to *play*.

Example 10

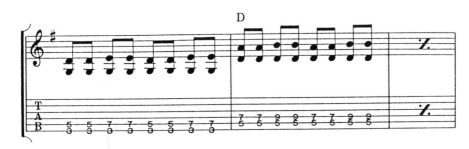

Example 10 presents the basic rhythm guitar style on which so many of Berry's greatest songs were built. Using G, C, and D major barre chords in the 3rd and 5th positions, you'll find this pattern easy to play and very useful—it's been one of the most popular in rock from the '50s through today. Use your pinky to fret the high notes on the second and fourth beats of each measure, and accent those beats slightly for that backbeat (you just can't lose it . . . .).

Example 11

Example 11 is a solo composed of Chuck Berry-style phrases and designed to be played over a rhythm pattern much like the one presented in Example 10. Again, almost every note falls comfortably within the G minor pentatonic scale at the 3rd position. The A sharp to B natural slurs are obtained by barring the B and G strings at the 3rd fret and hammering on to the G string's 4th fret with your middle finger.

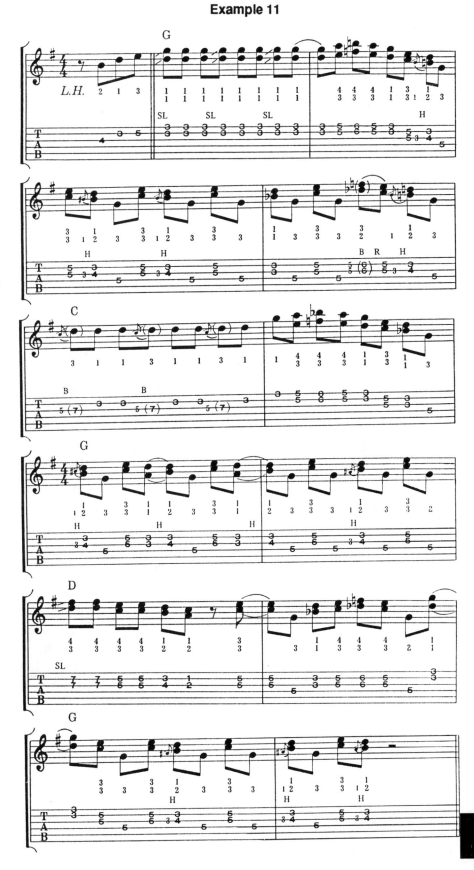

Moving On

Believe it or not, once you've mastered the pentatonic minor scale, the barre chord, the bend, and hammers and pull-offs, you've really got all the basic rock guitar techniques down, and you can at least *approximate* most of what you hear on just about any rock recording. From here on it's just a matter of perfecting your technique and developing your style—which can take a lifetime—and keeping abreast of new techniques, remaining open to future developments, and expanding your knowledge of music.

As mentioned before, the pentatonic minor scale appears in many configurations, not just the box position. Here are the fingerings for the pentatonic scale in the key of G minor, starting with the familiar box position at the 3rd fret:

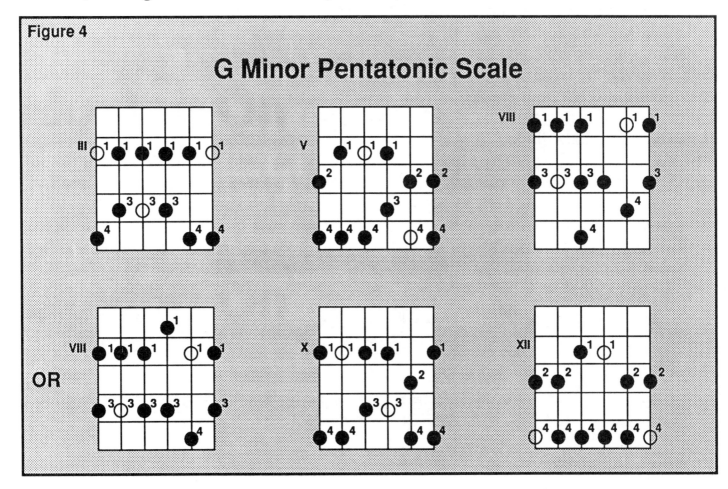

Figure 4

G Minor Pentatonic Scale

Example 12 should be filed under "Food for Thought." It's a simple lick based on a bend and a pull-off or two—but you'll notice that it features *two* lines of tablature. The upper tab line shows the fingering for the lick as you might play it in the 8th position, while the lower line shows the same lick in 12th position. The point is that you shouldn't get locked into one or two positions because you never know when you'll be in mid-solo and suddenly find yourself in unfamiliar territory. And most of the phrases and solos in this book (and just about anywhere else you find them) can be played, at least partially, in dozens of ways. The way that works for Steve Lukather, Elliot Easton, or G. E. Smith (file that under "Sneaky Ways to Mention Your Favorite Guitarists") just might not work for you, me, or the next guy. That's why no two guitarists ever sound *exactly* alike.

Example 12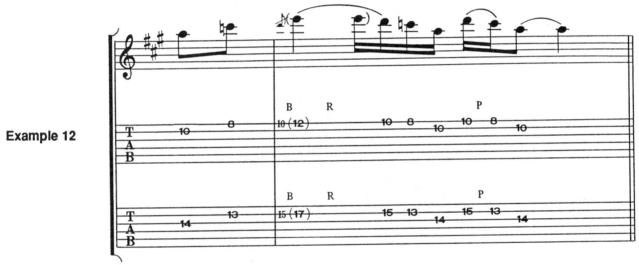

To see how easy it is to get around the fretboard when you're familiar with *all* the patterns, give Example 13 a try. A slow, bluesy lick that would probably be played unaccompanied, this example climbs from the low range of the guitar to the 15th fret through slides and position shifts. The grace notes introducing the 5th fret are much easier to play than they appear. They're slurred very quickly by sort of *brushing* the top three strings with a continuous downstroke, followed by a single upstroke into the bend. And remember the damping effect you got in Example 6 by lightly resting the heel of your hand on the strings? Use the same technique for the first six notes of measure 7 here. A quick listen to the taped version will make all this much clearer.

Gm Throughout

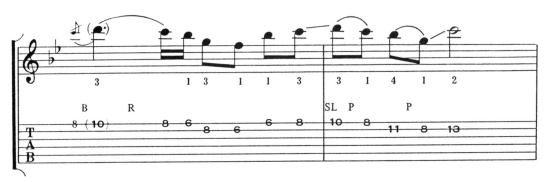

Example 13

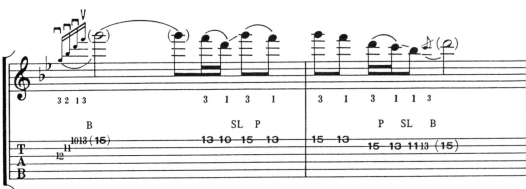

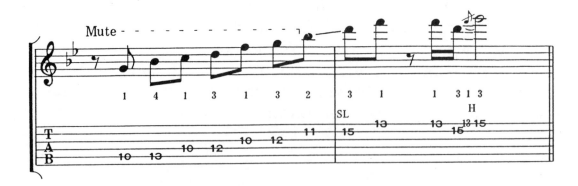

Example 14

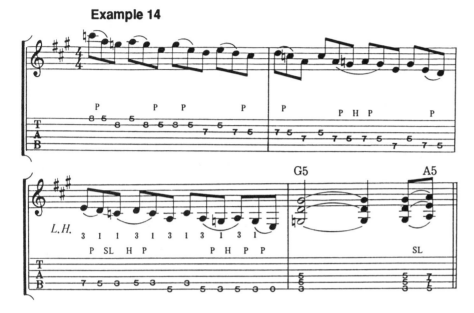

Examples 14 and 15 are four-bar cadenzas based on the A minor pentatonic scale. Example 14 ends with a conclusive-sounding power chord hit, but the ambiguity of the pentatonic scale and the A5 "chord" make this lick sound right over either A7 or A minor chords.

Example 15 is a great pull-off exericise that should have your left-hand pinky looking astronaut tough in no time.

Example 15

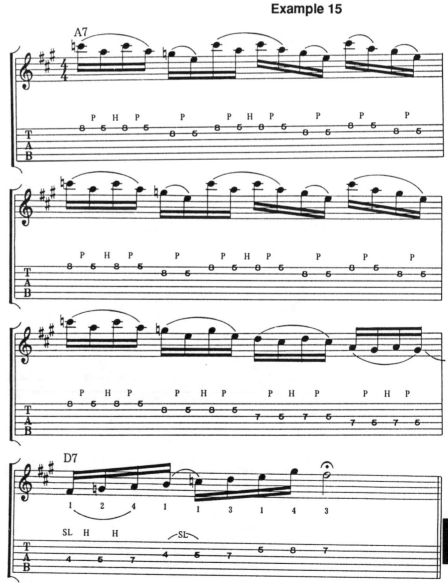

Example 16 is an eight-bar solo over the kind of chord progression you might hear in the middle section of a song. In C minor its home base is, as usual, the box position (this time at the 8th fret); but the chord changes dictate a slight divergence from the pattern in several places. You might think of this solo as alternating between the C minor pentatonic box and the F minor pentatonic scale in the 8th position.

Example 16

Example 17 is a funk rock rhythm pattern typical of the music of Jimi Hendrix, Stevie Ray Vaughan, and other blues-influenced rockers. It requires a freer right-hand wrist than the straight eighth-note patterns we've seen so far, and it uses an open low E string for that droning bass effect. The primary chord is an E augmented 9th chord—a 7th chord with a raised 9th on the top. The effect is a blurring of the major/minor tonality—and that's pretty much what the sound of the blues is all about.

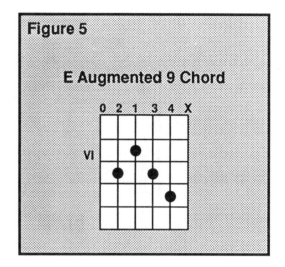

Note the use of the A5, G sharp, and G5 forms in the second and fourth measures. They are not really chord changes as such, and so they do not affect our choice of the E minor pentatonic scale for the solo (Example 18).

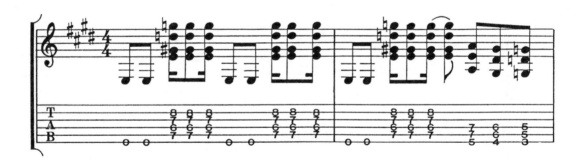

Example 17

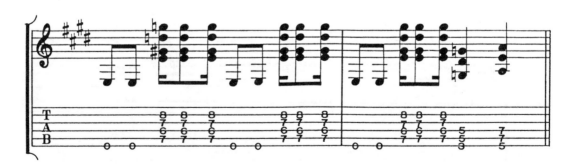

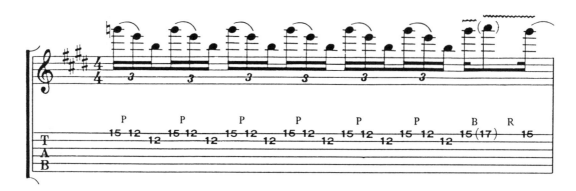

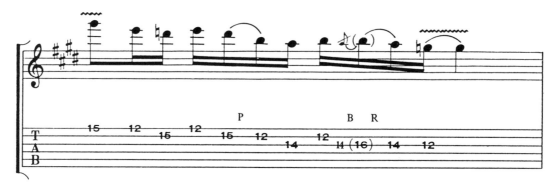

Example 18

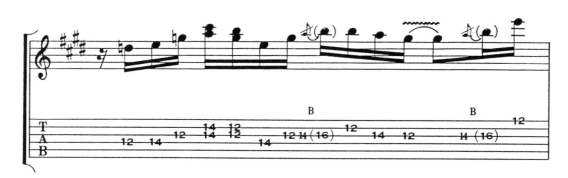

Example 19 is the kind of rhythm/lead alternating part you might be called on to play at the beginning of a rock arrangement—the guitar takes the lead, soloing up to the figure (the five chords in the last few measures) and then switches to a rhythm part while a vocalist or another instrument takes the lead. This example contains a little bit of just about everything we've covered up to this point, so be sure to pay close attention to the fingering directions and listen to the recorded version if you need any extra help.

Example 19

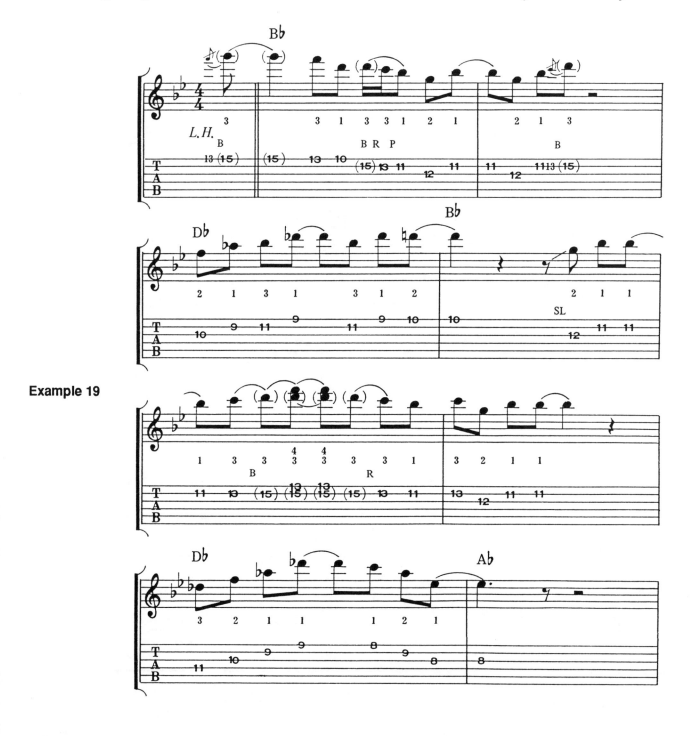

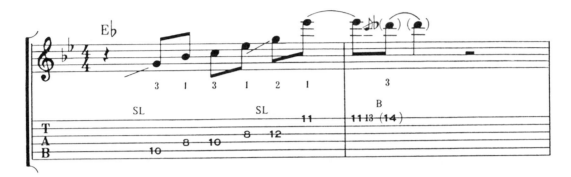

Example 19
Continued

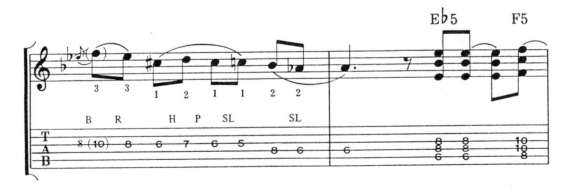

And Now for the Bad News...

It seems logical that the best way to become a good *rock* guitarist is to become a good *guitarist* or, more basically, a good *musician*. The chances are good that you've grown up listening to rock music, that you're familiar with its subtleties and nuances, that the sound itself is second nature to you.

But today's rock guitarist is better educated, more technically proficient, and more open-minded than ever before. It seems that all the young heavy-metal players are coming out of prestigious music schools like Berklee and G.I.T., and young guys best known as funk or R & B guitarists can play Wes Montgomery and Charlie Parker solos with amazing facility. Just look at any issue of *Guitar Player* Magazine—these days, Paganini is cited as an influence almost as often as Jimi Hendrix or Eric Clapton.

The best way I've found to develop technique is the most traditional. Even after years of playing, I still try to practice scales at least an hour a day—and always use a metronome.

On the next page are seven fingering patterns for the G major scale—each runs about two octaves and stays in one position on the fretboard—and the corresponding fingerings for the G harmonic minor scale, which is very popular among classically influenced players like Yngwie Malmsteen. Try playing each one from the bottom to the top of its range and then back again using alternating picking (that is, pick the first note with a downstroke, the second with an upstroke, and so on) and playing with the metronome set at a comfortable speed. Take your time, play the notes evenly and smoothly, and gradually you will find your speed, your control, and your self-confidence improving.

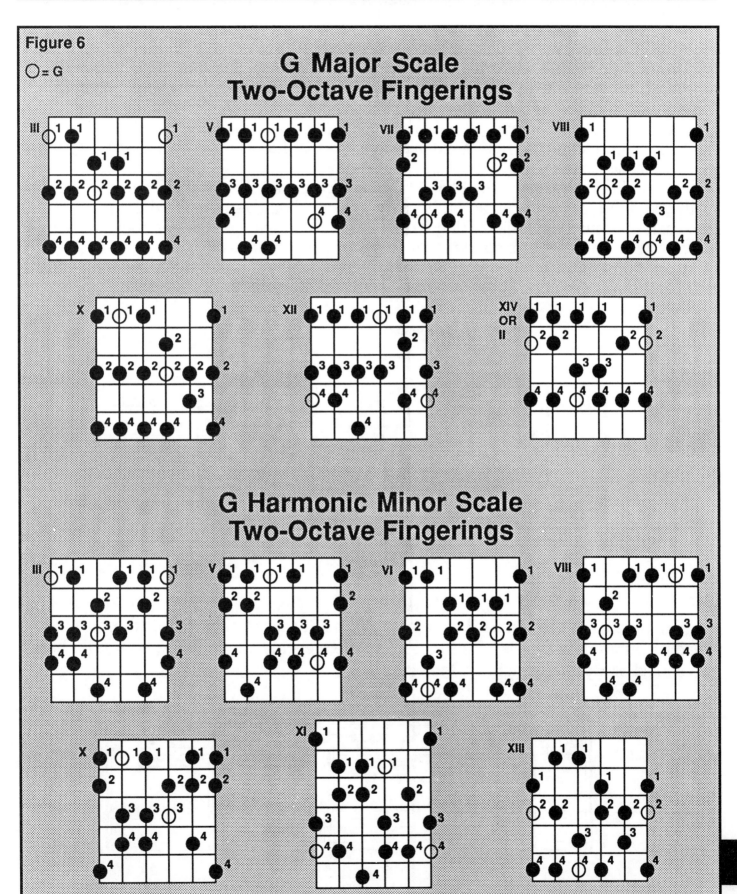

Figure 6

$\bigcirc = G$

G Major Scale
Two-Octave Fingerings

G Harmonic Minor Scale
Two-Octave Fingerings

Right-Hand Tapping

Ten years ago, many rock fans and critics had become bored with the "guitar hero syndrome," preferring bands featuring few or no solos, rejecting their predecessors' emphasis on virtuosity in favor of the emotional intensity they believed only technical primitivism could assure. And then along came Eddie.

A superb technician and yet a searingly emotive player, Eddie Van Halen is best known for perfecting the right-hand tapping style that has become as important to the rock guitar vocabulary as the bend or the pull-off.

Example 20 shows the right-hand tapping technique in its most basic form. Begin with your left-hand index finger at the 5th fret of the high E string. Hold the pick between the thumb and middle finger of your right hand and *tap* or hammer on to the E string at the 15th fret – using the index finger of your *right* hand. Then, again using your left hand, quickly pull off to the 5th fret and hammer on to the 8th fret with your left-hand pinky. You don't *even* need to *own* a pick to play this one.

Tap all circled notes

8va throughout

Example 20

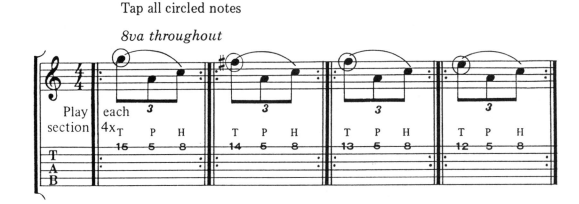

Example 21 is very similar to Example 20, but it uses straight sixteenth notes instead of eighth-note triplets. Be sure to play them evenly and in time—your right-hand tap should always occur right on the beat.

Example 21

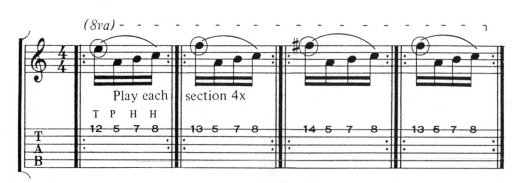

Example 22 is slightly more melodic. Again, the lick is played all on one string, but here the left hand moves from the 2nd to the 4th, 5th, and 8th positions. This lick is based primarily on the A harmonic minor scale.

Example 22

Example 23 introduces a twist—each of the first four groups of sixteenth notes is played on a different string.

Example 23

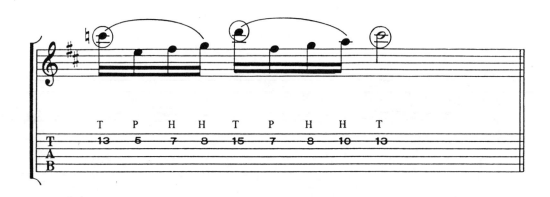

In Example 24, the first note is picked normally (or plucked by the right-hand index finger, if you prefer) and the tap occurs *off* the beat. Don't let the unusual rhythmic grouping throw you—just play the notes slowly and evenly, remembering that the lowest note of each group falls on the beat.

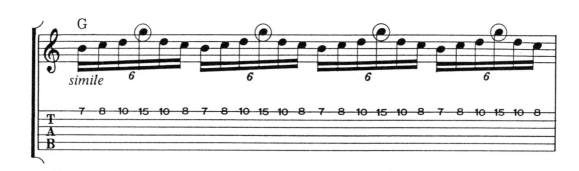

Example 24

Example 25 is sort of a reminder—you can obtain a great effect by tapping on to a note on a string that is already being bent, but remember to adjust the location of the tap to compensate for the bend. If you are bending the string enough to sharpen the fretted note a full step, tap two frets lower than you normally would to obtain a given note.

Example 25

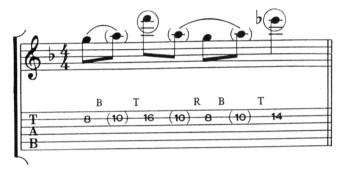

Remember the blisters, the discomfort you suffered during those first awful weeks of learning to play chords? Well, be prepared to undergo similar pains as your right-hand index fingertip develops a callus. But you got over it the first time, didn't you?

Like so many other techniques we've discussed, this one is most effective when used in conjunction with bends, trills, and standard left-hand hammer-ons and pull-offs. To many guitarists, the technique is an end in itself; but a study of the Van Halen style reveals a sophisticated sense of phrasing, tone, and solo development, with right-hand tapping an embellishment, a little "something extra," a means to play wide intervals and odd-numbered note groupings that might prove extremely awkward using standard methods. And it is a visually exciting move. But every effect, it should be remembered, must serve the music—not the other way around.

False Harmonics

A great way to add color to your playing is to use a technique very similar to right-hand tapping to produce a chiming, bell-like tone or an eerie, whistling effect. No doubt you are aware that lightly touching the strings at the 5th, 7th, or 12th fret without actually pressing them down mutes or "cancels out" the fundamental tone (the note you would hear if you were to cause the string to vibrate by picking or plucking it normally) but, thanks to the physical properties of sound, allows the *overtones* to ring. The sounds produced by this method are referred to as "natural harmonics."

Now, that's useful as long as you're interested only in the notes available as harmonics on the open strings; but you can get a similar effect by lightly touching the string *with some part of your right hand* directly above the fret one octave—twelve frets—above any note on the fingerboard. The sounds produced this way are called "false" or "artificial" harmonics.

As with right-hand tapping, I hold the pick between my thumb and middle finger, then lightly touch the string with my index finger while picking in as close to a normal fashion as this configuration allows. Try playing Example 26. The harmonic is indicated by a diamond-shaped note. Touch the string twelve frets above the indicated tablature position while picking.

Example 26

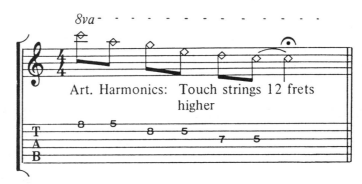

One of the greatest things about false harmonics is that they can be bent like any normally played note:

Example 27

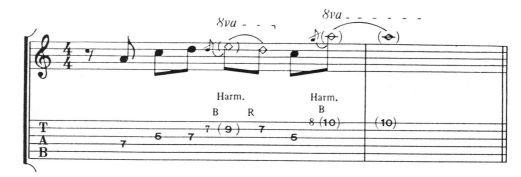

Many players achieve basically the same effect by gripping the pick tightly between the thumb and the index finger, allowing only the very tip of the pick to protrude, and striking the string simultaneously with the pick and the fleshy part of the side of the thumb. And I understand that Eddie Van Halen has a new technique (where have we heard *that* before?). Not surprisingly, he obtains false harmonics by *tapping* the string directly on the fretwire one octave above the fretted note, pulling the finger quickly away from the tapped fret (but not executing a standard right-hand tap or pull-off).

And here's a great trick I learned years ago from a pedal steel guitarist: Try getting a sweet, harp-like effect from a *full chord* by brushing the strings an octave above the chord position (and following as closely as possible the contour of the chord form) with the fleshy part of the *side* or *heel* of your right hand while strumming. To play Example 28, fret a standard A major barre chord at the 5th fret as you normally would, then pick the individual notes as indicated, allowing them to ring. Then, for the final chord, switch your pick back to its normal position between thumb and index finger and play the false harmonics as indicated with the heel or side of the right hand.

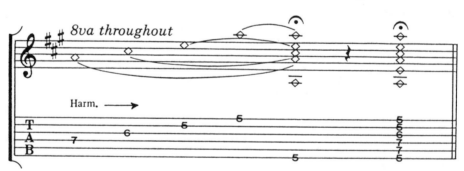

Example 28

A Parting Shot

Example 29 is a solo designed to touch on most of the techniques covered in this part of the book. At this point, it may prove challenging but not *too* difficult; and I hope you have fun with it. I've transcribed three choruses, but the tape goes on a little further. Why not try to figure out the rest yourself by listening to the tape?

Meanwhile, good luck and *keep practicing!*

First Chorus

Example 29

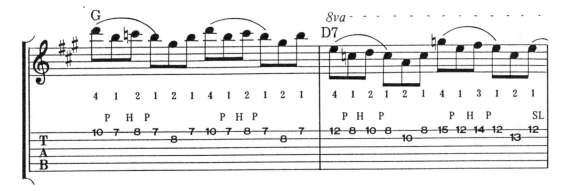

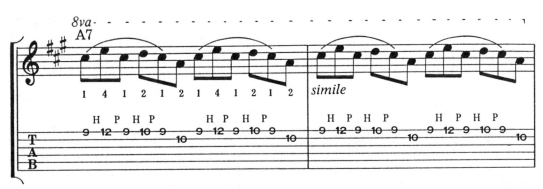

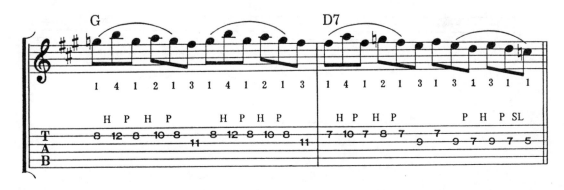

Second Chorus

Third Chorus

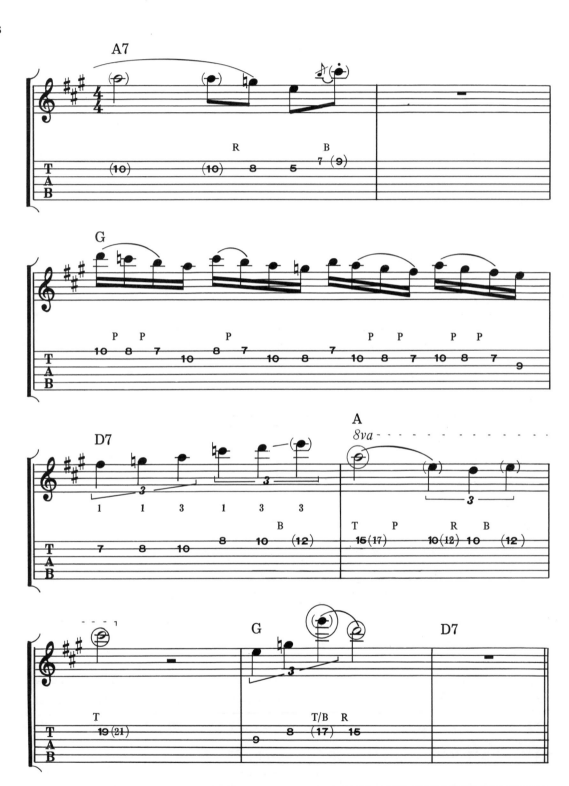

For further study, see Mel Bay's *Complete Rock Guitar Book* (MB94560).